I
pray
in
poems

I
pray
in
poems

Meditations
on Poetry
and Faith

DAVE WORSTER

 Morehouse Publishing
NEW YORK

Morehouse Publishing, 19 East 34th Street, New York, NY 10016

Morehouse Publishing is an imprint of Church Publishing Incorporated.
www.churchpublishing.org

Cover design by Laurie Klein Westhafer
Typeset by Rose Design

A catalog record of this book is available from the Library of Congress.

ISBN-13: 978-0-8192-3186-4 (pbk.)
ISBN-13: 978-0-8192-3187-1 (ebook)

Printed in the United States of America

I pray in words. I pray in poems.
I want to learn to pray through breathing,
through dreams and sleeplessness, through love and renunciation.
I pray in snow that falls outside the window.
I pray in tears that do not end.

From *In That Great River: A Notebook*
By Anna Kamieńska
Selected and translated from the Polish by Clare Cavanagh

Contents

Foreword: Saints and poets

Emily: Do any human beings ever realize life while they live it—every, every minute?

Stage Manager: No—Saints and poets maybe—they do some.

—"Our Town"

Try to imagine a member of your church saying something like this: "You know, I just don't like parables very much. They're difficult to understand. They never mean what I think they mean. I feel like parables always contain hidden messages that I don't quite get, and it takes someone with a degree in religion to explain them to me. They make me feel stupid, so why bother?" How would you respond to such a remark? My first impulse might be to point out that the disciples themselves were remarkably obtuse in the face of Christ's teachings, so if we do struggle to comprehend them, at least we are in some very good company. Many of us would probably also respond that sure, parables can be challenging, but experience has revealed to us that focused study of these stories yields effective and memorable lessons about life and faith. In other words, the parables offer a worthy return on the time and energy invested.

It may be easier to think of a friend or acquaintance saying something like this: "You know, I just don't like poetry very much. It's too deep, too difficult to understand. I feel like there's always a hidden meaning that I am not clever enough to discover. It's just not worth the effort." For twenty-two years as a classroom teacher, I've pushed back against this sentiment, facing down recalcitrant students and reluctant friends who decline to join me in my affection for metaphors and meter. With my brothers and sisters in the faith, I've maintained (religiously) that if parables are worth the effort, then poetry is too. The thing is, unless the person conversing with me happens to be enrolled in one of my classes, time and occasion rarely converge in such a way that I can whip out a sonnet from my back pocket, using it as evidence to prove, in five minutes or less, that poetry surely does repay the investment. Indeed, if I were ever to attempt such a ploy, I am positive I would become one of those parishioners you would avoid at all costs during fellowship hour coffee.

In fall 2013, some good folks at my parish, the Church of the Holy Family in Chapel Hill, North Carolina, gave me the chance to put my money where my mouth is. They invited me to give a couple of talks about poetry with themes appropriate for Advent. So I chose a hand-ful of poems, wrote up some discussion topics for each, and distributed all the material to the participants in advance. We gathered on the appointed Sundays, and near the end of the conversation about each poem I folded a relevant Bible verse into the mix. This strategy invari-ably precipitated additional thoughtful comments about the poem's beauty and meaning. These sessions were quite wonderful, a combina-tion of brief "professorial" remarks, lively group discussion, and spiri-tual meditation. We filled our classroom to overflowing each time, and several people asked me after the conclusion of the final session to lead another series soon. A year later I was asked to do so during Lent. If anything, the Lenten sessions attracted even more people. Given the strength of the response in my own parish, I found myself wondering if a wider audience might exist for a volume composed of meditations or reflections upon poetry and scripture placed side by side. What you hold represents the result of that pondering.

I offer this back story as explanation for some of the choices I have made herein; for instance, I've organized the poems according to the liturgical seasons of the Christian year because of the idea's origin in Advent and Lenten discussion series. As the book developed, inter-esting thematic implications of placing these "expressions of eternity" within a framework of time and the seasons also emerged. I have also included at the end of the book a set of discussion questions for each poem. I encourage brave Adult Education Leadership to organize gatherings perhaps along the lines I describe above. I offer the ques-tions free for the taking—hand them out, bring folks together, and see what happens! I hope, among other things, that this book will serve as a sort of "out-of-the-box" resource for Christian Formation programmers. You have everything here you need to put together seasonal poetry offerings.

I also hope the book will serve as more than just a set of resource materials. Much study, prayer, and conversation have gone into each offering. A teacher and student of poetry, I know that some of the observations I've made are original and unique, products of the unusual approach I've adopted of exploring each poem through a spiritual lens, even (or perhaps especially) those works that seem resolutely secular. To explore the theme of resurrection through the chiasmic structure of "Heron Rises from the Dark, Summer Pond" or to interpret "Those Winter Sundays" as a poem about foot-washing is to enter new interpretive territory, so I hope that all readers and lovers of poetry will find something to excite and inspire in the three or four pages of analytical reflection I've written for each work. Toward that end, and to aid those folks who have not at their immediate command the terminology of literary analysis, I've pulled together a list of poetic terms and placed it near the end of the book. I've kept it short, including only terms I felt necessary for understanding and appreciating the poems in this volume (actually, I've left one term in just for fun). Finally, I've included an early chapter sharing some possible strategies for reading poetry, again endeavoring to keep it brief and accessible. It precedes a detailed, step-by-step reading of a poem called "Advent" by Rae Armantrout.

A bookmark I received as a gift recently reads, "We cannot grow without a trellis." To all incipient poetry lovers holding this slim volume right now, I sincerely hope I have provided enough of a trellis so that you may grow and bloom in delight over the works that follow. For previously confirmed devotees, I pray the unique context of this study will provide new insight, fresh understanding, and satisfying, soulful conversations about some wonderful works of art composed by poets . . . and by saints.

With Gratitude

I gratefully acknowledge the parishioners of Church of the Holy Family who attended multiple poetry discussion sessions over the years and often provided wonderful ideas and insights. Three readers in particular reviewed the manuscript at various stages of production: to Sarah Ball-Damberg, Lisa Ray, and Lanis Wilson, my deepest thanks.

In April 2011, I was diagnosed with prostate cancer. I underwent surgery that same year, with follow-up radiation in 2012. For about six months in 2013, we thought we had the disease licked, but then the lab tests started showing a rise again in PSA levels. I am currently stage four, responding well to aggressive treatment and am at peace, mostly, with a prognosis that can be measured in years (God willing) as opposed to months or weeks. While not a book about a Noble Man Fighting Cancer, *I pray in poems* is a book full of choices made in the context of that fight. Shakespeare's "Sonnet 29," for instance, appears in this volume because I have been that persona, angrily jealous of friends whose lives are not structured around lab tests and clinic visits. "A prayer that will be answered" deeply moved me the first time I read it, not only for its frank confidence that we will all suffer and die, but also for its equally frank confidence that a day will dawn, someday, when all such suffering will end. Many other selections have illuminated the darkness in myself, never without some pain or shame, but always in the hope of healing. Perhaps some of these meditations will do the same for some of my readers.

Three men, all of whom share my struggle, have been especially compassionate and precious companions to me along this four-year journey fraught with fear, anger, and loss. At various times and in various ways, they have each offered me unique understandings of the physical, emotional, and psychological challenges we have shared. To

Eric, Ed, and Brian: thank you for giving so freely of your time and counsel. This book belongs in part to you.

Finally, along with the affection and support of my two children, Jen and John, the steadfast love and fidelity of my wife, Lisa Morris Worster, has been the rock on which I've rebuilt my damaged life over the past four years. I cannot imagine what kind of shape I would be in today without the refuge of her patience and devotion. Lisa, in this life you have been my poetry, my faith. I love you.

Expressions of Eternity
Ecclesiastes and Shakespeare

A FEW NIGHTS AGO, I was reading the Sonnets of William Shakespeare (why yes, for pleasure; I do that), and I encountered "Sonnet 15," which you'll see in its entirety a bit further on in this chapter. For reasons I could not at the time fully fathom, I immediately thought of the book of Ecclesiastes from the Old Testament. So I looked that up and read it, too.

I just love Ecclesiastes: You'll find nothing else quite like it in the Old Testament. This book announces its theme in its opening lines: "Vanity of Vanities, says the Preacher, vanity of vanities! All is vanity!" (1:2). Check out the New International Version of the same verse: "Meaningless! Meaningless!" says the Teacher. "Utterly meaningless! Everything is meaningless." How can you *not* love a book that starts like this? Our word "vanity," by the way, derives from a Latin term meaning "emptiness" or "nothingness," but apparently the original Hebrew word in Ecclesiastes also suggests "something as fleeting as a breath of air." Certainly, that just about sums up the Teacher's[1] attitude. We live lives brief and unsubstantial as a breeze, meaningless and soon forgotten.

Consider a few more passages from this fabulous book: "I have seen everything . . . under the sun and behold, all is vanity and a striving after the wind" (1:14, NIV). "For of the wise as of the fool there is no enduring remembrance, seeing that in the days to come all will have been long forgotten" (2:16, ESV). "For the fate of the sons

---

1. The author of Ecclesiastes (translated variously as "preacher" or "teacher") claims to be King Solomon, son of David. Many readers take that at face value, while others question this claim for various reasons. The question of authorship is neither here nor there for my purposes, so I intend to sidestep the controversy entirely, content to refer to the author as "the Teacher" and move on.

of men and the fate of the beasts is the same; as one dies, so dies the other" (3:19, NASB). And finally, "there is no remembrance of former things, nor will there be any remembrance of later things yet to happen" (1:11). Cheerful stuff, right? Just the ticket to curl up with on a gray, rainy Monday.

The good news in Ecclesiastes: What does the Teacher suggest we do other than wallow in the abject nothingness of existence? Think on God. Remember "your Creator in the days of your youth," admonishes the Teacher, "before the evil days come" (12:1; by "evil days," the Teacher means "old age"). Remember that "whatever God does endures forever," and, therefore, "Fear God and keep his commandments; for this is the whole duty of man" (3:14 and 12:13, ESV). Based on what I've offered so far, the central idea of Ecclesiastes could be stated something like this: "We lead brief, insignificant lives that will soon be forgotten. The only meaning available to us derives from the Word of God and the perspective that Word gives us." All well and good, but for me the message from this absolutely fascinating book becomes more complex the further I sink into it.

Take, for example, this passage: "There is a time for everything, and a season for every purpose under the heavens: . . . What do workers gain from their toil? I have seen the burden God has laid on the human race. He has made *everything beautiful in its time*. He has also *set eternity in the human heart*" (3:1, 9–11, NIV, emphasis added). Here, you see, the Teacher adds a couple of subtle wrinkles. For one thing, he suggests that the natural cycle of life, for all its futile, relentlessly repetitive emptiness, can also hold a God-given beauty and dignity. Chapter 3 contains the beautiful passages some will recall from a song written by Pete Seeger and recorded by The Byrds: "a time to be born, and a time to die; a time to plant, and a time to reap" and so on. In addition to the unpleasant dimensions of life we have grown to expect from the Teacher (death, weeping, war, hatred, and sexual abstinence), these nine or ten verses include the joys of planting, harvesting, laughing, dancing, making love, and having children. The years of our lives are brief, yes; but *totally* devoid of significance? Not so much.

The idea of Eternity: More important for my purposes, the Teacher acknowledges that God has planted the idea of eternity into the hearts of humankind. We may be incapable of fully comprehending this eternity, mind you, incapable of understanding *all* that "God has done from the beginning to the end" (3:11, ESV), but we *want* to. Metaphorically and literally, our eyes constantly scan the heavens, searching for the answers we hope to find there. Grounded in our material existence, we yearn still for that which will transcend it. This represents our human paradox, and its articulation in Ecclesiastes represents part of the reason this book holds a special place in my heart.

Faith represents one way, obviously one very important way, that we might attempt to access the infinity that lies beyond our finite existence. But other possibilities also exist. The Teacher asserts that God has endowed creation with beauty within the cycles of time, and so we might seek to perceive those touches of eternity in the world around us, feeding our faith on the experiences of everyday life. Or, inspired perhaps by the beauty of the natural world, we might even compose our own artistic expressions. Art (for me, poetry and literature, but I do not mean to exclude any Art) presents another means, perhaps, through which we might express the idea of eternity that God himself has planted in our hearts and minds.

The topic of Great Art brings us back around to, of course, William Shakespeare and, finally, to his "Sonnet 15":

> When I consider everything that grows
> Holds <u>in</u> perfection but a little moment,
> That this huge stage presenteth nought but shows
> Whereon the stars <u>in</u> secret <u>in</u>fluence comment;   *line 4*
>   When I perceive that men as plants <u>in</u>crease,
>   Cheered and checked ev'n by the selfsame sky,
>   Vaunt <u>in</u> their youthful sap, at height decrease,
>   And wear their brave state out of memory.   *line 8*
> Then the conceit of this <u>in</u>constant stay
> Sets you most rich <u>in</u> youth before my sight,
> Where wasteful time debateth with decay
> To change your day of youth to sullied night;   *line 12*
>   And all <u>in</u> war with time for love of you,
>   As he takes from you, I <u>en</u>graft you new.

For those of you who find a first reading of the sonnet tough sledding, please don't abandon hope! In the next two paragraphs, I'll explain enough so that you'll see the connections back to Ecclesiastes. By the time I ask you to go back and reread it, most of the sonnet will make a lot more sense, I promise you.

I find the number of similarities between this sonnet and Ecclesiastes really quite remarkable. First, the sonnet establishes a context of **the natural, vegetative cycles** of the world: the speaker of the sonnet, also called the *persona*, considers "everything that grows" and perceives that men also increase (grow) like plants. The persona also observes that **youth is fleeting:** all growing things hold "in perfection but a little moment," and people "vaunt in their youthful sap," but from that "height" inexorably decrease. This **inevitability of decay** is further developed in lines 11 and 12: "Where wasteful time debateth with decay / To change your day of youth to sullied night [of old age]." (We can read the word "debateth" in line 11 as meaning something like "works together," since Time and Decay are clearly conspiring against the "day of youth.") We saw all of these ideas also articulated by the Teacher.

In a final connection to Ecclesiastes, the sonnet's persona imagines our lives as empty performances ("this huge stage," earth, presents nothing but empty "shows") that will **soon be forgotten.** We wear our "brave state," or theatrical costumes, beyond the time when anyone will remember us ("out of memory"). Shakespeare, by the way, develops this bitter metaphor further in a famous speech by Macbeth: "Life's but a walking shadow; a poor player / That struts and frets his hour upon the stage, / And then is heard no more. It is a tale / Told by an idiot, full of sound and fury, / Signifying nothing" (5.5.24–28). "Utterly meaningless!" says the Teacher. "Everything is meaningless."

In both Ecclesiastes and "Sonnet 15," we are posed a question: How do we make meaning for these meaningless lives? How might we transcend the relentless drumbeat of the dreary days? As we have seen, the Teacher advises that we turn to God, for only what God renders will truly last forever. Shakespeare takes us in a different direction. In the final couplet of "Sonnet 15," the persona declares himself "in war with time" and assures the youth to whom he has dedicated the poem that, as time "takes from you, I engraft you new."

"Engraft" represents the key term in the sonnet. Its primary meaning: to replace the dead branches of old trees by inserting a scion (or shoot) from another tree, which then grows into a new branch. As such, this term participates perfectly in the "cycle of life" metaphor that dominates the poem. The persona promises the youth in line 14 that "as time strives to wither you, I renew you through engrafting." How the persona intends to accomplish this renewal lies imbedded in a pun on "engraft," which can also be read as *in-graph*. The root word *graph* derives from the Greek term *graphein*, "to write," and thus a second, simultaneous reading of line 14 might be "as time strives to wither you, I renew you by writing this poem." Pretty neat, huh?

The sound of "engraft": I could go on (and on) about "Sonnet 15," but for now I'll settle for a final observation about that key term. The first syllable of "engraft" (Shakespeare spelled it "ingraft") represents a recurring sound in the sonnet. We hear *in-* at least eight times before we reach line 14. (I've underlined them in the poem above for your convenience.) On the other hand, the *–aft* letter combination occurs nowhere else in the poem. In context, the second syllable's unique sound underscores the idea of novelty we register as we read the sonnet's final word. Do you see this? In a single word, "in-graft," the poet has attached a completely new sound to a repeated, familiar sound. Shakespeare has accomplished a linguistic engrafting simultaneous with his literary one. This is just astonishing. It's the kind of detail I point to when somebody asks me "What's the big deal about Shakespeare, anyway?" (Now try going back and reading the poem again.)

"Sonnet 15" happens to be the first in a series of what some critics call Shakespeare's Immortalizing Sonnets, those that claim the power to preserve forever though poetry the object of the persona's love. The most well known of these may be "Sonnet 18" ("Shall I compare thee to a summer's day?"), the final two lines of which go like this: "So long as men can breathe or eyes can see, / So long lives this [poem], and this gives life to thee." In these lines, the persona promises the youth that his "eternal summer" shall never fade as long as these words survive for the eyes of humankind to read and to remember. To extend the theme of these sonnets, I would argue that *all* poems "immortalize," all are "in war with time." German poet Paul Celan once wrote that a poem "can be a message in a bottle." The poet puts feeling to paper and sets it adrift in the hope that one day a future wanderer will find it washed up upon the shore. The life of the written word thus endures.

Expressions of eternity: According to Christian theology, the birth of Jesus represents the one moment when the eternal divine penetrated into human history. That birth (and subsequent death and rebirth) provides those of us in thrall to time access, through faith, to a world beyond the threshold of death. To the extent the life of Jesus represents God's plan for our salvation, that life is a work of art, made manifest in the writings of the New Testament. Christ, the Word incarnate, the Author of our Salvation, also carries a message in a bottle. Centuries later, we, those wanderers on the shore, receive that Word and (God hopes) clasp it with cries of joy. If the verse from Ecclesiastes represents a promise ("He has also set *eternity* in the human heart"), then the life of Jesus fulfills that promise ("everyone who believes in him will not perish but have *eternal* life," John 3:16, New Living Translation, emphasis added to both lines). Faith, like poetry, is an expression of eternity. Just as all poems, regardless of subject matter, project hope into the future, faith also finds itself in war with time as our belief encourages us to focus our gaze beyond sinfulness, strife, and suffering to the hope of a better life to come. In this world, we can find meaning in both the Word and the words. Faith is a kind of poetry; poetry, a kind of faith.

READING POETRY
"Advent," by Rae Armantrout

IF POETRY IS A KIND OF FAITH, then reading poetry, like growing into faith, will not come without its challenges. Over time, I have found that learning to enjoy poetry can be, for some, a bit like being a Christian: hard work (sometimes *very* hard work), but so worth it in the end. I believe that confronting an opaque work of art is not unlike tackling an obscure Bible verse (or a puzzling parable), and just as understanding scripture brings with it a certain pleasurable insight, so too can we make a joyful noise when we see why George Herbert structured his poem "The Collar" just so. I hope you will find that, like living a life in faith, living a life in poetry, while perhaps initially intimidating, gets easier the more you practice. I offer now a few tips on the practice of reading poetry in the spirit of 2 Timothy: "God has not given us the spirit of fear; but of power, and of love, and of a sound mind" (1:7, American KJV). Read poetry boldly! Don't let it daunt you! You have already had a taste of poetry courtesy of William Shakespeare. In this chapter, I offer a challenging contemporary poem. Please read my suggestions below, take a deep breath, and jump into Rae Armantrout's "Advent."

Look at your poem: The well-known naturalist and Harvard professor Louis Agassiz was famous for a unique pedagogical strategy. As described in an essay by Samuel H. Scudder, Agassiz instructed him (Scudder) to gaze for hours at a specimen of a fish in a tin tray, encouraging him continually to "*look* at your fish! O, look, look!" In the spirit of Agassiz, I say to you, do not underestimate your own powers of simple observation. *Look* at your poem! What do you *see*? How has the poet organized the words and lines on the page? Is one line of poetry longer or shorter than the others? Do you see any isolated or repeated words or phrases? Does the poet use *italics* or **bold font** or ALL CAPS anywhere? Pay attention to any patterns you perceive or variations on those patterns. The appearance of the poem on the page will provide signals for an understanding of it.

Listen to your poem: Many of us pause and offer prayers before we read the Bible. We ask God to clear our minds so that we might better understand and appreciate his word. While not explicitly suggesting you pray before you read a poem (though some of you may want to), I do advise that you pause, close your eyes, take a deep breath or two perhaps, and clear your mind. This isn't an email in front of you here, or a tweet; it's a work of art. It requires a certain level of attention. Despite this mental preparation, please don't expect to understand the poem from beginning to end the very first time you read it. You might, but you probably won't, so anticipate (in every sense of the word) that you will need to go through it a few times. Whenever possible, read the poem out loud so that you can literally hear the words, their sounds, and their rhythms. Good poetry teachers often compare poems to songs: The first time you hear a song, you usually don't catch it all, right? You miss some of the lyrics, sometimes the words at the beginning of the song don't make sense until you hear what follows later on, and often you need to listen to it several times before you feel like you really "get it." Think of poetry the same way, and relax. "Listen" to the poem several times.

What draws you in? Remember that a skilled poet deliberately chooses words and phrases that will create images and ideas. Take note of those by focusing on details that either appeal to you or seem meaningful. Does a particular line intrigue you or create a picture in your mind? Or maybe you just like the way it sounds when you read it out loud? Zero in on that and ask yourself why you are drawn to it. Also, ponder the title of the poem. You've got to figure that the poet has given some thought to that title and it provides information regarding what the poet, at least, thinks should command your attention in the lines that follow.

It's all about the journey: If you approach a poem with the goal of arriving at a final, definitive destination, you will likely be thwarted. It may surprise you to learn that often—*very* often—poetry leaves some issues unresolved. Like life itself (and faith), some questions might remain unanswered, and some conflicts remain in suspension. Paul writes in 1 Corinthians that now we see as through a glass, darkly; and sometimes you will feel this way about poetry. Rather than see this as a source of frustration, embrace it as a kind of liberation. The poet has not created a work with one single meaning and with all tensions resolved. This means the reader may take certain liberties to participate in the making of meaning. So consider a reading of a poem as more of an exploration or a conversation and less as a mining expedition. Avoid thinking, "I just *know* I'll find THE meaning of the poem in here somewhere, if I just keep rummaging around." Instead, try thinking, "What does this poem have to say to me, and what do I have to say in return?" For the purposes of this volume, you could also ask, "Is this poem a prayer?" If so, what is the persona trying to say to God? What does she hope to hear in return?

I mean none of the above to suggest that I won't share with you some additional strategies along the way to help you further understand some of the truly wonderful works of art that lie in store for you in the pages that follow. For one thing, I've provided a list and (usually) brief explanations of some of the poetic terms I use in this book. Again, I don't intend this glossary to intimidate, but rather to empower. After all, when you journey through a foreign country, you do better if you know some of the lingo. I don't recommend you read the list now or commit it to memory (there will be no quiz at the end of the chapter). Instead, I suggest you wait until you encounter an unfamiliar term later on in the book, then flip to the glossary and look it up (I've italicized all glossary terms in the book); thus, you'll acquire the definition of the term just as you are looking at an example of it in a specific poem.

A special note about persona: Imagine each poem as being spoken by a character created by the poet. We call this character the *persona*, and all readers must understand this very important point: *we cannot assume the persona equals the poet.* You may have noticed that even as I was writing about Shakespeare's "Sonnet 15," the speaker of which identifies as the author of the poem, I still did not make the assumption that this first-person voice was Shakespeare's. Think of the speaker instead as a creation of the poet, like a character in a play. If you were to imagine the poems in this collection as a set of monologues delivered by fictional characters, you would not be off the mark. To reinforce this vitally

9

important concept, I have deliberately throughout the book adopted for each persona a third-person pronoun of the gender opposite that of the poet (so if the poet is male, I assume the persona is female). You'll see only one or two exceptions to this practice, which I will note as we get to them. Further, because each poem is spoken by a *persona*, we can often identify a tone of voice. Sometimes the tone will seem fairly straightforward, even neutral, but often the tone will sound angry or sad, sarcastic or ironic. So some of the most important questions you can ask of a poem are: Who is speaking? How would you describe this speaker? Can you discern the context within which the persona speaks? How would you describe the tone of voice? Sometimes some of these questions will seem next to impossible to answer, but if you can answer even just one or two of them, you gather helpful information.

By the way, understanding persona provides another reason why it's helpful to read the poems out loud: you may find capturing a tone of voice easier if you do so. Understanding persona also helps us grasp how poems can often be deliberately imperfect. Just as playwrights often create flawed and complex characters, poets often create flawed and complex personas. So keep in mind that the speaker of the poem may have a limited point of view or an incomplete understanding of the situation. She may also be overwhelmed by a particular emotion, or she may be harboring unresolved tensions or inner conflicts. Indeed, since I propose that all the poems in this volume touch upon matters of spirituality or faith, unresolved tensions, inner conflicts, and unanswered questions are practically guaranteed. The persona may feel angry, frustrated, or confused, and if the poem can be interpreted as a prayer, the persona may be expressing all this emotion to God. Just as in real conversation (and real prayer), communication may sometimes feel awkward, incoherent, or ambiguous. You might not always understand everything the speaker has to say. Don't make that the goal.

Finally, poetry usually addresses a meaningful aspect of life or human experience: "Meaningful" is in the eye of the beholder. Something vitally important to *me* may have little or no significance for *you*. I get that, but I do think most readers find that most good poetry touches upon human emotions and relationships, our experiences with the natural (or urban) world around us, or how we go about composing a "meaningful" existence during our brief time here. As the discerning reader will have no doubt surmised by now, I have chosen poems for this volume which I believe offer provocative, insightful, or challenging words about our relationships with God. Often, these poems take as their subject, specifically and clearly, faith, but sometimes they do not. At least not specifically or clearly. I do believe, along with the Teacher of Ecclesiastes, that God has planted the idea of eternity into every human heart and every human mind. With surprising frequency, even when the topic is not explicitly faith, the poetry gestures towards ideas that transcend or endure: how fear can paralyze; how grief can bury; how love can transform; and how beauty can inspire. As I have done with Ecclesiastes and Shakespeare, I will bring together these various expressions of eternity, the words (of the poets) and the Word (of God). I have found these intersections illuminating and inspiring. As you take this spiritual walk with me, the poets, and the saints, I hope you will think so too.

BEGINNING: "ADVENT" BY RAE ARMANTROUT (2009)

In front of the craft shop,
a small nativity,
mother, baby, sheep
made of white
and blue balloons.   *line 5*
    *

Sky
     god
         girl.
Pick out the one
that doesn't belong.   *line 10*
    *

Some thing
close to nothing
         flat
from which,
fatherless,
everything has come.   *line 16*

As an exercise in how to approach a poem, I offer the following four exploration questions, based on the section you have just read above. Please answer these four questions on your own before proceeding to read the rest of what I have written:

1. Look at "Advent." What do you see?
2. Read the poem several times. Write questions about anything you don't understand.
3. Focus on what draws you in. Jot down what you find interesting and why it interests you.
4. Who is the persona? What is the persona's tone of voice?

1. Look at "Advent." What do you see?

When you look at a poem, you will see a form, pattern, or structure. Sometimes, the poem will take on a recognizable shape, and you will see lines of poetry clustered into groups called *stanzas* with words arranged to conform to a rhythmic and/or rhyming pattern. Sometimes the poem doesn't conform to a conventional structure like a four-line stanza or a sonnet. This doesn't mean that the pattern isn't there; it does mean that the poet has elected to create a unique structure, one suited to the artistic purposes of this particular work. Every poet deliberately decides which words to use, the order of those words, where to end one line of poetry, where to begin the next line, and where, if ever, to skip a line to create divisions or subsections within the poem. Assume every choice means something.

When I look at the structure of "Advent," I note several things. Clearly, the poem defies any conventional expectations about poetic form, for it doesn't manifest a regular pattern of any kind, nor does it break down into recognizable, uniform stanzas. The first five lines all have about the same length, so they *look* like a stanza, but we see no rhyming pattern. A white space and asterisk separate these first five lines from the next five, which look very little like the first five. Lines 6–8 consist of a single word each ("Sky" coming at the beginning of line 6, "god" in the middle of line 7, and "girl" at the end of line 8), followed by two more lines before another separation (and another asterisk). The final section is six lines long, and two of those lines consist of single words, "flat" and "fatherless." These two words appear connected by *alliteration*. Through this detailed observation, we can discern that the poet has divided the poem into three parts; that several words are apparently emphasized by their isolation on a line; and that lines 6–8, if read from left to right, create a descending movement. No doubt, you made some of the same observations, in addition to some others I haven't listed. So far, so good.

2. Read the poem several times. Write questions about anything you don't understand.

After reading the poem at least three times, write down questions that you think need answering in order to come to an understanding of the work. Please do this exercise realizing (and accepting) that you will *not* actually come up with all the answers, and further, that having a couple of unresolved questions in your mind will *not* detract from your enjoyment of the poem.

Here's my list of questions:

Why begin the poem in front of a craft shop?

Why only three figures from the nativity? Why no Joseph, no Magi, no other animals, etc.?

Is the word "sheep" plural or singular?

Are all three figures made of white and blue balloons, or just the sheep?

Why balloons? Why white and blue?

    *

Why those three particular words: "Sky," "god," and "girl"?

Why each on a separate line?

Why does the persona tell us to pick out the one that doesn't belong?

Which one doesn't belong?

    *

Why is "some thing" separated into two words? Why not "something"?

What does "close to nothing" mean?

Why is "flat" given a line all to itself?

What does "everything" refer to?

Why are the sections divided with an asterisk instead of just white space?

Undoubtedly, your lists contain further questions, but these will be more than sufficient for starters, especially since we have no intention of answering them all.

3. Focus on what draws you in. Jot down what you find interesting and why it interests you.

Here's another tip: you don't need to answer your questions in order. Feel free to jump around. Sometimes understanding something later in the poem will suddenly illuminate a puzzling point in an earlier section. I find the middle section of "Advent" the most compelling part of the poem because it contains an explicit command to the reader: choose the one that doesn't belong. So I'll begin there. Which of these three words doesn't belong with the other two? Well, "god" and "girl" both begin with the letter "g," so I might choose the word "sky." But wait, "sky" and "girl" are both part of creation, while "god" suggests divinity, so I might choose "god" as the term that doesn't belong. One might even argue, since many of us associate "god" with heaven (in the "sky"), that "girl" is the odd term out. What do we make of this? Since a reasonable argument could be made for any one of the three choices, perhaps that means the persona has no single correct answer in mind. It really is up to the reader. Could *participation* be the key to understanding the poem?

In that context I go back to the first section and my first question. Why begin the poem in front of a craft shop? Is "craft shop" yet another suggestion of participation or creativity? After all, this nativity scene has been *made* by somebody, right? And now I have a possible answer to the next question: why only three figures (unless "sheep" is plural)? Because the creator of this particular nativity scene, for whatever reason, made that *choice*. I can now imagine the first section, with its image of a very specific nativity, as a kind of response to the command

14

of the second section: pick what you think does and does not belong. I further note that the nativity includes mother, child, and animal(s), but it excludes the male figures. No Magi, no Joseph; it is, in the word of the final section, "fatherless." I can't answer any of the other questions for this first section yet, but I will note that blue is a color often associated with the Virgin Mary, and white, with purity or divinity.

Finally, I drop down to the questions for the final section. I find this section, with its repetition of that vague noun "thing," to be the most puzzling, so I'll share another strategy with you: sometimes I find it helpful to write out lines of poetry as if they were sentences. So I tried that with this section, and here's what it looks like:

"Some thing close to nothing flat from which, fatherless, everything has come."

This helps a little. It seems to me now that the words "close to nothing" and "flat" modify that "some thing" from which "everything has come." Two commas separate "fatherless" from the rest of the sentence, and it seems to modify "everything." In the context of the rest of the poem, "fatherless" makes me think of Jesus, the baby from the first section, he who lacks an earthly, biological father. So my evolving understanding of the sentence now stands as:

"Some thing close to nothing flat from which, fatherless, Jesus has come."

From whom did Jesus come into the world? Perhaps Mary, the girl from the middle section and the mother from the first? So maybe this final section presents an image of "Mary, from whom, fatherless, Jesus has come"? Not the only possibility, of course, but I will go with that for now and move on to the persona.

4. Who is the persona? What is the persona's tone of voice?

I'll confess right up front that I see little in the poem that provides contextual clues. It's tough to identify who or where this persona is (male? female? young? old? in any particular place?). Rather than get hung up on it, I'm just going to move on to tone of voice. Read the first five lines out loud. To my ear, at least, the tone seems quite neutral in this section. These first lines describe an image in language that seems fairly straightforward and uncharged with any particular emotion. As I read the next five lines, though, it seems to me that a hint of playfulness enters the poem. The persona lists three nouns, and then asks the reader to pick the one that doesn't belong with the other two. It's like a word game. It reminds me of the bit from the old *Sesame Street* TV shows where "one of these things is not like the others." Having said this, I must also add that some readers won't see that shift in tone at all, reading the final two lines of the second section of the poem as more straightforwardly declarative. Reading tone is not always easy, and there's often not one "correct" way to interpret it.

But if you agree with me on the playful tone, then perhaps you'll also hear that tone continuing into the next section? Going back to my questions, why is "some thing" separated into two words? Perhaps to emphasize the repetition of that second word? We see it again at the end of the next line ("nothing") and again in the final line ("everything"). To me, this repetition echoes the cleverness of a really good riddle ("I am something close to nothing from which everything has come. What am I?"). As was the case with the middle section, the persona seems to be asking the reader a question: what, or who, is "some thing"? My answer to the question is Mary, Mother of Jesus, but that might not be your answer.

Let's pause here and assess. As you will have undoubtedly noticed, we haven't answered all the questions we've asked about "Advent." That's okay. It could be that we have answered enough, though, to come to one understanding of the poem. "Advent" offers three distinct versions of the nativity, two of which, at least, compel the reader actively to participate in creating that nativity. By logical extension, this interpretation suggests that we all construct our own nativities, if you will. We all come to our own understandings of what Advent means to us, what Christmas means to us, and what God means to us. Faith requires active engagement.

I think this poem is about creative participation. Yes, Armantrout entitled the poem "Advent," which means a beginning or an arrival, but this "Advent" also embodies an act of creation that takes its place in a spectrum of ongoing creation: past ("from which everything has come"); present (the nativity in front of the craft store and, perhaps, the poem itself); and future ("pick out the one that doesn't belong" prompts a response yet to come). That final line of the poem reminds me of the words from the Gospel of John: "In the beginning was the Word, and the Word was with God, and the Word was God. . . . all things were made through him, and without him was not anything made that was made" (1:1–3). Thus we might also perceive the presence of Jesus throughout the poem: the "baby" of the first section, the "god" of the second, and the "everything" of the final line, through whom all things were created.

Oh, and what about that seemingly innocuous detail of an asterisk between stanzas? Why not just leave an empty space? Is this choice random or does even the asterisk have meaning? Well, what does an asterisk look like? What shone over the manger on the night of Christ's nativity? Just a thought. It turns out that there's a lot going on in this little poem, but notice that it hasn't really been all *that* difficult to get a handle on it. Subsequent chapters will focus much less on step-by-step analysis and much more on content, but you should answer the four questions I outline above before you read each meditation. They will take you a long way towards composing your *own* understanding of the poetry in this book before you read what I have to say.

A final note about the poet: You may find it useful or interesting to know that Rae Armantrout practices what has been called "Language Poetry." This term may puzzle you perhaps, at first; after all, isn't most poetry "language poetry"? Yes, but the expressed purpose of language poetry is to call attention to language as a cultural construction in and of itself. Words have meanings, and we have rules regarding how we can put words together in sentences that also have meanings. "Language poetry" defies those conventions and breaks those rules. Language poetry pushes against denotation, encouraging . . . nay, forcing the reader to engage actively in the making of the poem's meaning.

I have elected to begin with Armantrout's poem in order to borrow a page from the language poet's philosophy and set a tone for this book. As I have taught poetry over the years, I have realized that many students don't like poetry because they believe there exists some secret code that unlocks the hidden meaning. Often, readers get so bound to their own preconceptions of poetry as difficult or esoteric or "too deep for a regular person" that they cannot just relax and let themselves experience the work on their own terms: what *they* see in the poem or the questions *they* want to ask. So I wanted to start with a poem that so clearly demands that readers participate. You can't really come to an understanding of "Advent" (the poem) unless you actively engage in it. I strongly encourage you to participate on the same level with each poem in this volume and, by extension, with the spiritual dimensions of your life each poem invites you to explore. You can't really come to an understanding of Advent (the season) unless you actively engage in it. Or Christmas. Or Lent, or Easter. Your faith is an ongoing act of creation.

THE SEASON OF ADVENT AND
THE CASTLE OF PERSEVERANCE

AT SOME POINT IN GRADUATE SCHOOL, I had the distinctly dubious pleasure of reading a fifteenth-century morality play called *The Castle of Perseverance*. I remember the play for two reasons. Reason 1: Linguistic scholars have somehow determined that the good folk of the late Middle Ages pronounced "perseverance" with the accent on the second syllable, per**sev**erance, instead of how we pronounce it now, with the accent on the third syllable, perse**veer**ance. I don't know how they figured that out, but I am very glad they did. Our modern pronunciation seems less pleasing to me somehow, with that unpleasant *sneer* of a *veer* right smack in the middle of the word. I thought then, and still think now, that the older pronunciation flows more easily off the tongue. Don't you agree? Per**sev**erance, to rhyme with **rev**erence. Nice, yes? While I long ago abandoned my one-man crusade to change the word's pronunciation, this kind of thing greatly occupied my mind in my graduate student days. Still does, I suppose: the sounds of language matter to me ("engraft"!). I surely could not write a book about poetry otherwise. Reason 2: *The Castle of Perseverance* is the only play from its time period that comes down to us with a drawing that offers some insight into how it might have been originally performed. I like drama very much, and I like set designs very much, and though I don't care much for *The Castle of Perseverance*, the set design for this play I found very interesting indeed.

The Castle of Perseverance reads more like symbolic allegory than compelling portrayal of characters in conflict and resolution (though given that the stakes were eternal life or damnation, it undoubtedly amounted to pretty gripping stuff in the 1400s). In the play, a character called Mankind, a symbol of . . . well . . . all mankind, engages in a struggle to remain virtuous in a sinful, fallen world. From Mankind's birth, he has arrayed against him characters called Greed and Pride and Lust-loving (not just Lust, mind you, lust-*loving*) who tempt him away from other more virtuously named characters like Shrift and Penance and Chastity (you know, the types you really want to ring up on a Friday night). Well, the play (*thousands* of lines long), while sometimes still performed today, really presents a challenge to the patience of modern readers. I certainly found it tedious and unbearably pedantic, but as I've said, one rather crudely rendered drawing I recall to this day.

Original performances of the play likely took place outside, in what may have been a "theater in the round" mode. In the center of the drawing, we can clearly see the tower-like Castle of Perseverance itself, with Mankind's bed underneath it, surrounded by a narrow moat; around the castle appear five "scaffolds" or raised platforms, each identified with a particular entity or place (Belial, The Flesh, The World, Covetousness, and, to the east, God).

As the play unfolds, we witness several interesting staging effects. For example, at a certain point in the play, we find Mankind ensconced in the Castle of Perseverance, under attack from various Vices; the Virtues repulse these adversaries by tossing rose petals (symbolizing the Blood of Christ). Later in the play, after Mankind dies in his bed, an actor playing Soul comes out from under that bed (where he has been the entire time!) to play his role. (The notation under the castle in the drawing reads: "Mankind's bed shall be under the castle, and there shall the soul lie under the bed till he shall rise and play.") Finally (and here's the moment that has really stayed with me), after over three thousand lines of dialogue, suddenly, almost out of nowhere, we hear the voice of God. The play provides scant stage directions, so perhaps in early productions the actor playing God did enter at some point just prior to his lines, but the text contains no positive evidence to support that possibility. God speaks from her[1] scaffold, and this speech could suggest that she has been perched there, perfectly visible and

---

1. Believing that God should not be limited by our narrow gender conceptions, I will use both male and female pronouns when referring to her.

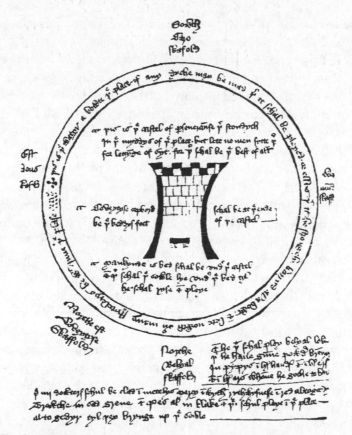

Staging *The Castle of Perseverance*: Directionally, the drawing is upside down. South ("Flesh's Scaffold") is at the top, and North ("Belial's Scaffold") is at the bottom. The three words to the extreme left read "East Deus' Scaffold," where God apparently sat for the duration of the play.

apparent to all other characters (including Mankind), from the very first moment of the play. In other words, God has been quietly present all the while, but Mankind could not, or *would* not, see her. And here's what I find particularly intriguing about the scenario: Does this staging of the play suggest a way of understanding our complex relationship with God? Then and now, I gaze at this unsophisticated, yet wonderful set design and think to myself, over and over, "Huh. Through all the uncertainty and spiritual tug of war, God was present with Mankind all along, literally right before his very eyes."

The season of Advent: I've recalled *The Castle of Perseverance* frequently as I have read poetry and written the sections of the book for Advent, Christmas, and Epiphany. From the sudden and unexpected voice saying "child" in "The Collar" to the touch of grace in "Love Poem," I've been struck repeatedly by the presence of God in these works, often in ways entirely anticipated (the Christ Child in "Journey of the Magi," for instance), but also sometimes in ways quite unexpected. Advent recognizes the coming of Christ as a light in the chill darkness of winter, and one important theme of the season is joyful, hopeful anticipation. Yet you will also note how frequently the speakers of these poems, frustrated by the apparent lack of something in their lives, impatiently abide in the deep silent darkness until the presence of God finally makes itself known. In Shakespeare's "Sonnet 29," "myself almost despising" expresses the self-loathing of an impatient soul; the persona in "The Oxen" wistfully imagines returning to a barn at midnight; and the speaker of "Bezhetsk" slams the door on terrifying memories of the past. The light approaches, but until then we grope blindly in the shadows.

"I pray in poems," writes Polish poet Anna Kamienska. Like Kamienska, we need help finding the courage to embrace the entirety of our material existence: both the dreams and the sleepless nights; both the peace of quiet snowfall and the tears that do not end. Many of the poems that follow are prayers to the light, attempts to speak into the waiting silence. They sometimes express gratitude and wonder, sometimes doubt and fear, but to each prayer I find the answer returns: I love you. I am here. Always.

Advent Meditation I
"The Collar" by George Herbert (1633)

I struck the board*, and cried, No more.
                    I will abroad.
        What? Shall I ever sigh and pine?
My lines and life are free; free as the road,
        Loose as the wind, as large as store.   *line 5*
                    Shall I be still in suit*?
        Have I no harvest but a thorn
        To let me blood, and not restore
What I have lost with cordial fruit?   *line 9*
                    Sure there was wine
        Before my sighs did dry it: there was corn
        Before my tears did drown it.
        Is the year only lost to me?
                    Have I no bays* to crown it?
No flowers, no garlands gay? All blasted?   *line 15*
                    All wasted?
        Not so, my heart: but there is fruit,
                    And thou hast hands.
                    Recover all thy sigh-blown age
On double pleasures: leave thy cold dispute
Of what is fit, and not. Forsake thy cage,   *line 21*
                    Thy rope of sands,
Which petty thoughts have made, and made to thee
        Good cable, to enforce and draw,
                    And be thy law,
        While thou didst wink* and wouldst not see.
                    Away; take heed: *line 27*
                    I will abroad.

23

Call in thy death's-head* there: tie up thy fears.
He that forbears
To suit and serve his need,
Deserves his load.   *line 32*
But as I raved and grew more fierce and wild
At every word,
Me thoughts I heard one calling, *Child!*
And I replied, *My Lord.*

board: a table
in suit: waiting
bays: a crown of laurel leaves
wink: close your eyes
death's-head: a skull; a reminder of death

Before you read any further, I encourage you to read the poem several more times and work through the four steps outlined on page 12, or you can use the discussion questions about the poem on page 121.

Introduction to George: George Herbert definitely had a way with words. In addition to being a gifted poet, he is known for a wide variety of proverbs and pithy sayings such as: "living well is the best revenge," "good words are worth much and cost little," and "his bark is worse than his bite." Born into a wealthy family in 1593 (John Donne dedicated his Holy Sonnets to his mother, Magdalen Newport Herbert, because of her patronage), the well-educated Herbert dabbled briefly with a political career, but fortunately for us it was not to be. Following his own heart, Herbert married in 1629 and took Holy Orders for the priesthood the following year. Considering his wealth and connections, students are often surprised to learn that Herbert happily settled down and served a small, quiet parish exceedingly well as rector for three years. Sadly, he died of consumption (tuberculosis) in 1633 at the age of 40. All of his poetry appears in a single volume called *The Temple*, published in 1633.

The title: Knowing Herbert's profession, an almost irresistible image of the speaking persona forms in the reader's mind as we register the title of the poem. Does the speaker wear a priest's collar? Most of us can imagine only with some difficulty a cleric articulating the extreme frustration we hear expressed in this work. And yet, most readers find

24

"startling" and "powerful" two perfectly appropriate adjectives for much of Herbert's poetry, and "The Collar" presents a great example of Herbert's use of structure within which to explore authentic, chaotic human emotion. We hear an immediacy, an urgency in the voice that compels us to read on. We can relate to frustrated desires, and if an ordained priest can find herself chafing within the perceived limitations of faith's collar, then how much more understandable is it for mere layfolk like you or me? (Of course I realize Herbert was a priest, and thus we will be very sorely tempted to assume the speaker of this poem represents the poet himself. We should avoid this temptation, so I persevere in my decision to imagine the persona as the gender opposite that of the poet.) By metaphorical extension, we can understand this priest's collar to represent any kind of constraint, and in the second half of the poem we will see clear references to the cage, ropes, and cables the persona currently feels confine her. Finally, Herbert's audience would have heard in the title a pun on a word virtually unknown to us today, "choler," which means "anger" or "ill temper."

Crazy structure: After the title, the apparent lack of structure may be the next thing most readers notice. I mean, lean back in your chair and look at this thing! It's a mess! The left margin is not justified, and to say that line lengths vary would understate the case. We see no regular rhyme pattern, no stanzas. Nothing seems ordered or balanced. This apparent lack represents Herbert's deliberate choice, of course, and one of the things I most admire about the poem is the tension between the actual order apparent in the poem upon closer inspection and the emotional chaos contained therein. For example, since you are still leaning back in your chair, look at the poem again. Do you see the center line? The first words of all the shortest lines stack up at the same place, creating a visual sense of a plumb line dropping straight down through the heart of the poem. Can you see how that line becomes more visually pronounced as we get closer to the bottom of the page? To me, this suggests that, for all of the persona's wild and angry words, for all her fierce protestations that she will be free, she, like the poem, has a center. That center will hold, and she will return to it by the poem's conclusion. In fact, I would argue that the more the speaker seems determined to leave, the more resolutely the poem's structure reassures us that she will do no such thing.

Herbert brilliantly communicates this reassurance not only through the center line but also through the poem's elusive rhyme pattern. ("Rhyme pattern? What rhyme pattern?") Read "The Collar" again and note that the poet carefully pairs every single line in the poem with at least one rhyming line further on. Sometimes we have to wait for this couplet completion, but it always, always comes. Once again, apparent lack dissipates upon closer inspection. For instance, take the word "pine" at the end of line 3; it rhymes with "wine," but we have to wait seven lines before we hear it. The word "me" at the end of line 13 rhymes with "thee," but it takes a full ten lines to get there. For both these cases (and many others), until we do get there, the poem holds us in a kind of suspension: When will we hear the rhyme? When will this separated couplet be complete? This suspension/resolution pattern perfectly captures the overall tension of the poem. The speaker declares that she's had enough, and she swears she's leaving . . . yet she does not depart. We work our way through the poem to find out what will happen, to resolve our suspense. The rhymes come thicker and faster as we draw closer to the end, and by the time we get to the final four lines, well, something that looks a lot like a stanza appears, a regular *abab* rhyme pattern has been restored, and form has emerged from the chaos. Just beautiful.

Here's something we can all agree on: This persona is frustrated in the extreme. From the very first line, she strikes the board[1] and cries "No more!" Most of the remainder of the poem, right up to line 32, represents one long, ranting monologue. I find it a bit difficult to get a handle on the precise nature of the grievance, but clearly the persona thinks she has worked very hard and has precious little to show for it. Not for her any Ecclesiastical "the race is not to the swift, not the battle to the strong" nonsense. She communicates her frustration that she has "wasted" a year with nothing in return, no harvest to reap, no bay (laurel) leaves in recognition for her accomplishments, no flowers, no garlands gay, nothing. And it's not as if she hasn't been asking: she declares herself "still in suit," still waiting for the reward she has requested or that she obviously believes she deserves. As the poem opens, sick of cooling her heels, she

---

1. Lines 11 and 12 in the poem make reference to wine and corn. If one sees in those references an allusion to the Eucharist, then the board, or table, that the persona strikes could be imagined as the altar—rendering this initial image even more arrestingly powerful.

angrily declares that she's finished waiting and about to walk out. "I will abroad," she cries, longing for the freedom and the "store" (abundance or cornucopia) to which she feels entitled.

Before she leaves, though, she has much to say in at least two different modes. The first sixteen lines of "The Collar" I call the interrogative section (check out all the question marks), and the next sixteen lines I call the declarative section. Filled with strong active verbs like "recover," "leave," and "forsake," in this second section the speaker emphasizes her resolution to depart. Not coincidentally, most readers find this section far less comprehensible than the first one. For instance, note the pronoun confusion: the speaker shifts from a consistent first person singular in the interrogative section to a mixture of first person ("I will abroad"), second person (many uses of thy and thou), and even third person ("He that forbears") in the declarative section. I think the mishmash of pronouns indicates a profound internal conflict. Part of her wants to leave, but part wants to stay, too, surely. Otherwise, why does it take so much verbal expenditure to convince herself to go? In fact, it seems as if the closer the speaker gets to actual departure, the more psychologically fractured she becomes.

The persona herself acknowledges this lack of cohesion: "But as I raved and grew more fierce and wild / At every word. . . ." (lines 33–34). She's out of control, and she knows it. What pulls her back from the brink? The voice of the Lord answering this prayer. Herein lies the central irony of the poem: one single word silences and counteracts all the prior Hamlet-esque outpouring of words, words, words. With that utterance, the speaker remembers that, as a child of God, she is loved. Especially given the season, she (and we) might also recall and anticipate the Word made flesh, God's begotten child, the Word to answer all our words.

Two final observations: My favorite moment in the poem? Lines 7–9. At this early point, the persona still rants about her forlorn state: "Have I no harvest but a thorn / To let me blood, and not restore / What I have lost with cordial fruit?" She means this question as a complaint, but consider this: As soon as I read "thorn" and "blood," I think "crucifixion." In that context, when I read "restore," I think "resurrection," and when I see "cordial fruit," I remember the words of Paul in 1 Corinthians: "But in fact Christ has been raised from the dead, the first fruits of those who have fallen asleep" (15:20). Do you see this? Even as the persona gripes about her *apparent lack*, she subconsciously articulates this greatest of gifts: "have I no harvest but the crucifixion and resurrection of Jesus, through whom what I have lost has been restored?" No, you have no harvest but this. But what further harvest do you need?

Finally, say the title of the poem one last time: "The Collar." Now, read the last two lines out loud. Do you hear the echo? How does it change the orientation of the poem if we think of its title as "The Caller"? Like the character of God in *The Castle of Perseverance*, the Caller has been present in the poem from its beginning, waiting patiently for his chance to speak, for his chance to break through and to bring love to a broken life. And here we find ourselves right back to that experience of eternity within our numbered days. Here we find the abiding presence we wait and hope for this season, even, or especially, in the bleakest hours.

In Galatians, chapter 6, Paul extends the seasonal metaphor we have seen in Ecclesiastes to make a spiritual point: "whatever a man sows, that he will also reap. . . . he who sows to the Spirit will from the Spirit reap eternal life. And let us not grow weary in well-doing, for in due season we shall reap, if we do not lose heart" (7–9). In due time, the faithful will reap eternal life, but the persona of "The Collar," weary of well-doing, desires her reward now, on *her* schedule, and in accordance with the selfish desires of her own material existence. Like the Teacher of Ecclesiastes, she wearies of her toil, tired of restrictions, tired of self-sacrifice, and tired of forbearance. Impatient, she makes certain demands of God, and God has not answered those prayers. In her rage, she has forgotten God's promise. I warrant every single Christian, living or dead, has felt this way at one time or another. We have all cried out to God, with the psalmist: "Turn your ear to me; when I call, answer me quickly" (102:2, NIV). I know I have. I have been this priest, striking the altar, screaming: "Seriously?! After all that I have done for you, *this* is what I get in return?" In the hard-breathing silence that follows, I think I hear one calling. So God reminds us that in due season we shall reap the reward for our service, but it will come in his time: "You are my child, I am with you, and I want only what is best for you, so do not lose heart." Wait. Listen. Have patience. Persevere.

Advent Meditation 2
"Sonnet 29"
by William Shakespeare (1609)

When in disgrace with fortune and men's eyes,
I all alone beweep my outcast state,
And trouble deaf heaven with my bootless* cries,
And look upon myself, and curse my fate,   *line 4*
    Wishing me like to one more rich in hope,
    Featured like him, like him with friends possessed,
    Desiring this man's art, and that man's scope,
    With what I most enjoy contented least;   *line 8*
Yet in these thoughts myself almost despising,
Haply* I think on thee, and then my state,
Like to the lark at break of day arising
From sullen earth, sings hymns at heaven's gate;   *line 12*
    For thy sweet love remembered such wealth brings,
    That then I scorn to change my state with kings.

bootless: futile; something done in vain
haply: fortunately, with connotations of "happily"

Before you read any further, I encourage you to read the poem several more times and work through the four steps outlined on page 12, or you can use the discussion questions about the poem on page 122.

Sonnet structure: As we begin by just looking at the poem, I think we can all agree on one thing: Shakespeare's "Sonnet 29" is a *sonnet*. (If you are unfamiliar with the form and haven't read the glossary entry for *sonnet* yet, by the way, you may want to do so now.) The vast majority of sonnets written in the western tradition focus on a single subject in its myriad manifestations: love. Often, though by no means always, the *persona* speaks to or about the person he or she loves (called "the beloved" or the "love object"), and the sonnet portrays or reveals something about that relationship. In a nutshell, "Sonnet 29" shows us the transformative power of love. Early in the poem, the persona dwells upon that which she thinks she lacks in her life, but then she remembers that she is in love (and is loved in return), and this recollection restores her sense of well-being. The structure of the sonnet participates in its meaning. The word "When" introduces the first eight lines (two *quatrains*) of the poem. These lines describe the persona's distressed frame of mind at the poem's outset. The word "Yet" signals the start of the transformation (the "turn" of the sonnet, also sometimes called the "volta") at line 9; the persona suddenly thinks of her loved one, and her mindset dramatically shifts. Finally, the word "For" at the beginning of line 13 initiates a brief reflection upon how remembrance of her beloved reminds her of the riches she already possesses.

On Shakespeare and faith: In many ways we observe this persona on a very straightforward journey. Once we get a handle on the structure of the sonnet and the meaning of one or two archaic vocabulary words, the poem really poses few obstacles to an understanding as I've described it above. Having done so, though, I think it's fair to ask why I offer this poem in the context of Advent. Unlike Herbert's "The Collar" or Armantrout's "Advent," nothing in the sonnet (and nothing we know about this poet) really compels us to interpret it within any kind of faith framework. During his lifetime, Anglicanism represented the official Church of England, but Shakespeare left behind no journals or letters or any other direct evidence to suggest what his personal religious beliefs may have been. And even if he did hold personal religious beliefs, very few of Shakespeare's sonnets feature overtly religious, never mind Christian, themes or images. So why "Sonnet 29" in an Advent sequence?

Here's why: Conventionally, we would interpret the person referred to in line 10 of the sonnet ("Haply I think on *thee*") as . . . well, a *person*, the love object of the persona who, in this case, loves the persona right back (not always the case, alas). This interpretation certainly works and very much meets our expectations for a love sonnet. But what if the beloved referred to is not a person at all—what if it's God? Now, I freely admit that nothing in the poem *requires* this interpretation, but on the other hand, nothing explicitly *forbids* it, either. For me at least, the references to a place called "heaven" and the singing of "hymns at heaven's gate" constitute fairly overt religious imagery. This context of hymns and heaven creates a space within which a spiritual interpretation does not violate the sonnet and actually transforms it in significant and meaningful ways. For instance, this context might enable us to see more clearly the word "disgrace" in line 1 as suggesting a state of "dis-grace," out of relationship with God, a spiritual alienation that lends more weight to the "deaf heaven" referenced just a couple of lines later. This understanding in turn renders the metaphorical redemption and flight upward to sing hymns before the gates of (previously deaf) heaven later in the sonnet all the more startling and powerful. Well. Keep reading. You can buy the faith-based interpretation or not.[1] Either way, a central idea of the poem remains the power of love to transform covetousness and envy into praise and thanksgiving. Not a bad theme for Advent.

Nailed back into herself: The first *quatrain* of the sonnet paints a bleak picture of isolation. The persona feels like an outcast, "all alone" and in dis-grace with both "fortune" and "men's eyes." She feels alienated from heaven as well. The sonnet is a prayer, a cry to a heaven she thinks deaf to her bootless cries for relief from loneliness and despair. We see dark, negative inwardness through the first seven lines as the persona looks upon herself and curses her fate. She hates her life. To use a phrase deployed by Mary Oliver (see "Heron Rises from the Dark, Summer Pond" on pages 104–5), this persona is "nailed back into" herself, rendered inert and imprisoned by negative feelings of jealousy and self-loathing. As you read the first several lines, I will bet that one of your questions went something like: "Why is the persona so down on herself and her life?"

---

1. At least one notable Shakespeare scholar, Stephen Booth, accepts with no fuss whatsoever that "[t]he Christian distinction between material and spiritual well-being functions as a hyperbolic metaphor throughout this sonnet" (180). Booth goes on to note on the same page that the love described in lines 9–12 functions in the same way as "the love of the deity does in Christian theology." So there you go!

As we move into the second *quatrain*, note how the persona seems firmly mired in a sense of her existence as oriented horizontally. We can easily imagine her sullenly peering about on all sides, feeling surrounded by others whom she perceives as better looking or more popular or more talented or smarter, and wishing she were more like them. Her jealousy desires *that* person's good health, *this* person's beauty, *that* man's circle of friends, and *this* woman's artistic abilities. She wallows in covetousness, so much so that this sin may be, in fact, why she feels alienated not only from deaf heaven but also from all the others around her. I mean, as a fellow human being, how much fun could you have in the company of such a malcontent? No wonder she feels lonely and isolated, but she doesn't yet realize that her miserable state is self-inflicted. Almost literally, she has cursed herself.

A hint of the epiphany to come lies in line 8 (I love this): "With what I most enjoy contented least." The line concludes the speaker's litany of dis-possession while it simultaneously, albeit very subtly, indicates that the persona does indeed have something in her life that is usually a source of joy. She almost subliminally references this without realizing it, a signal to the careful reader that a change of heart may be on the horizon. (By the way, I also love the line for its sheer artistry. The perfect balance between the opposing ideas of "most enjoy" and "contented least," of abundance and lack, beautifully embodies in miniature a central idea of the poem as a whole.) In fact, the very next line foreshadows a person poised for this change of heart: "In these thoughts myself *almost* despising" indicates that she hasn't gone quite far enough in her despair or self-loathing to be beyond redemption, a redemption she recalls as her veil of self-pity and ingratitude finally falls away.

Movement: The most dramatic moment of the poem occurs in line 11, as the persona remembers her beloved, and then suddenly her state of mind, like a lark, soars upward through the sky in order to sing hymns of gratitude before the gates of heaven. The movement or orientation of the poem shifts startlingly in this line from sullen horizontal glares to exultant vertical flight. And here's one of the coolest things about this sonnet: note that line 11 is the only line not *end-stopped* (it does not conclude with a comma, period, or semicolon; this lack of terminal punctuation is called *enjambment*). Her joy so overwhelms the persona that she cannot contain herself within the structure of expression. Her emotion must overflow freely, like a cup running over. Her earlier, bitter prayers have become hymns of praise and thanksgiving at the gates of heaven, and it no longer matters if heaven hears or not. She now desires nothing more than what she knows she already has. That's quite a change from earlier in the poem.

One of the key words in the entire sonnet is "remembered" in line 13, "For thy sweet love *remembered* such wealth brings." The important point to make here: the love (in my reading, God's love, but really, any steadfast love) hasn't gone anywhere. The persona has possessed it all along, she just lost sight of it as she stumbled about in her fog of self-pity. I think again of the dynamic of *The Castle of Perseverance*. In that text, you'll recall, God has been present and imminently visible (yet somehow also invisible) to all characters, including Mankind, throughout the course of the play. Similarly, the persona of "Sonnet 29" has let her apparent lack blind her. She thinks that she is all alone, but she's not. She thinks she has nothing to be grateful for, but she does. She just has to remember it. If I were to ask you for a concise theme for the sonnet, "transformative love" presents an obvious choice, but one could also do much worse than "temporary amnesia." We could say the persona journeys from forgetfulness to remembrance, and as she remembers, she finds herself set free from the envy that nailed her down, free to look *up* instead of just *askance*.

How easily we might condescend to the persona of the poem: what a dolt! How can she *forget* a love that so thoroughly transforms her state of mind later in the sonnet? Further, the opening of the sonnet ("*When* in disgrace . . .") suggests a repeating cycle of forgetfulness. But we also might try to see ourselves in her. I know I do. As I have struggled with my health-related issues in recent years, I, like the persona in Shakespeare's sonnet, have sometimes looked upon myself and cursed my fate. I have perceived others as "more rich in hope," and I have wished myself more like them. And then, perchance, I look up at some pictures I've hung on the wall of my office. Our wedding day. My two children. A recent trip to San Francisco. And so I remember. Remember how blessed I am, how loved I am by my family, friends, and God, and how that knowledge renders every other thing immaterial. I believe we all occasionally dwell upon the perceived injustices of our lives. We harbor jealousies and discontents that imprison us in the same place where the persona finds herself at the beginning of this sonnet. So we need our weekly reminder, echoed in line 13, of a love that directs us to scorn the wealth and power of kings in the hope and promise, especially during this season, of the riches waiting for us in a very different kingdom: "Do this for the remembrance of me." So Shakespeare's "Sonnet 29" turns out to be an Advent poem after all. During this season of rampant consumerism and materialism, do not let temporary amnesia take hold. Remember what we wait for.

A final observation: I said at the beginning of this piece that we see no evidence in the sonnet compelling us to read it as overtly Christian in its message. I stand by that, but I also cannot help but point out that lines 11 and 12 could be read as subtle allusions to Christ's resurrection and ascension. If you allow a chain of logic which takes us from "break of day" to "sunrise" to "son rise," and if you layer over that an upward movement from sullen earth to heaven's gate, then we might hear a little whisper (*He is risen!*) of the light which will follow the darkness, but just a whisper. For Second Advent, as we look forward to the Rose Candle, a whisper is enough. (We will encounter a similar daybreak image in Anna Kamienska's "A prayer that will be answered," by the way. There's something to look forward to.)

In Romans, chapter 8, Paul writes: "Who shall separate us from the love of Christ? Shall trouble or hardship or persecution or famine or nakedness or danger or sword? . . . No, in all these things we are more than conquerors through him who loved us. For I am convinced that neither death nor life, neither angels nor demons, neither the present nor the future, nor any powers, neither height nor depth, nor anything else in all creation, will be able to separate us from the love of God that is in Christ Jesus our Lord" (35–39, NIV). Paul assures us that no material conditions, indeed, nothing in all creation, can disconnect us from eternity, but Shakespeare's "Sonnet 29" suggests an answer to Paul's initial question. Nobody can separate us from the love of God . . . except *us*. Our self-centeredness, our jealousy, our absent-mindedness, and our ingratitude can indeed distract us from the recollection of this love, always available to us for the asking . . . provided we *remember*.

THE ROSE CANDLE

"Love Poem"
by John Frederick Nims (1947)

My clumsiest dear, whose hands shipwreck vases,
At whose quick touch all glasses chip and ring,
Whose palms are bulls in china, burs in linen,
And have no cunning with any soft thing   *line 4*

Except all ill-at-ease fidgeting people:
The refugee uncertain at the door
You make at home; deftly you steady
The drunk clambering on his undulant floor.   *line 8*

Unpredictable dear, the taxi drivers' terror,
Shrinking from far headlights pale as a dime
Yet leaping before apoplectic streetcars—
Misfit in any space. And never on time.   *line 12*

A wrench in clocks and the solar system. Only
With words and people and love you move at ease;
In traffic of wit expertly maneuver
And keep us, all devotion, at your knees.   *line 16*

Forgetting your coffee spreading on our flannel,
Your lipstick grinning on our coat,
So gaily in love's unbreakable heaven
Our souls on glory of spilt bourbon float.   *line 20*

Be with me, darling, early and late. Smash glasses—
I will study wry music for your sake.
For should your hands drop white and empty
All the toys of the world would break.   line 24

I encourage you to read the poem several more times and work through the four steps outlined on page 12, or use the discussion questions about the poem on page 123.

The Rose Candle: If you have never marked the unfolding of the season through lighting Advent wreath candles, you have missed a warm and colorful tradition. Typically, an Advent wreath holds five candles, three purple, one pink (or rose colored), and one white. On the first two Sundays of Advent, the first two purple candles are lighted, symbolizing a focus on penitence and preparation. On the third Sunday, we light the rose candle to mark a transition in emphasis to joy and anticipation. This middle candle has always symbolized for me the rose that blooms midwinter. (Just to complete the sequence, on the fourth Sunday, we return to purple, and a white Candle in the middle of the wreath is reserved for Christmas Day.) For this, our third Advent meditation, I offer you a rose-colored Advent gift of pure joy, a poem by John Frederick Nims that deserves to be much better known.

Wild and crazy love: One would hardly expect a love poem to begin "my clumsiest dear," and one of the sheer pleasures of this poem is its unpredictability. Since the persona signals a clear and decisive departure from the "My Love Is Perfection" posture, we don't quite know what to expect from him next (note that since the beloved of the poem is likely to be female—you'll see a reference to "lipstick," for example—I am breaking my persona-as-opposite-gender-from-the-poet rule). As you may notice as you read the poem out loud, the poet keeps us continually off-balance with his uses of *enjambment* and *caesura*, not to mention surprising terms like "shipwreck," "fidgeting," "clambering," and "undulant." Look closely at the first eight lines: the first three have a natural, comfortable rhythm and are *end-stopped*, but when we get to the end of line 4, the lack of punctuation forces us to leap across the white space onto line 5, which pulls us up shortly with a colon. Line 6 also flows into line 7, where we find ourselves again

36

halted midline by a semicolon. By the time we make it to line 8, we can be forgiven for feeling a little seasick ourselves. The poet carefully creates discomfiting rhythms: the phrase "all ill-at-ease fidgeting" actually fidgets, just as "clambering on his undulant floor" really undulates. No wonder vases shipwreck with all this rollicking movement.

Notice also how our range of vision zooms in and out. I particularly admire how the persona imagines his "unpredictable dear" shrinking away from distant headlights yet leaping in front of nearby streetcars; similarly, she is a wrench in both the nearby clock and in the entire solar system. Time and space dizzyingly expand and contract along with the poem. Only as the persona moves into the fourth stanza, which describes when the beloved moves at ease or expertly maneuvers, does the rhythm itself also settle down.

Love's unbreakable heaven: In a poem filled with unexpected twists and turns marked by sudden words like "only" and "except," one of the biggest surprises is line 16. Up to this point, the poem has focused on the beloved, but here suddenly the scope of the poem expands again as we encounter an entire community of people devoted, along with the persona, to this endearingly awkward woman. In the wonderful penultimate stanza, the persona encourages us to imagine a circle of friends withstanding inadvertent personal attacks—coffee spilled on their laps or lipstick "grinning" on their coats—and persevering in the relationship for the sake of this otherwise kind and adorable companion. The two best lines of the poem offer fantastic rhythm and sound:

> "So gaily in love's unbreakable heaven
> **Our souls on** glory of spilt **bourbon float.**"

Beautiful! All those open "**O**"s help us hear with reinforcement how souls float in glory. These lines transcend all that has come before them, suggesting that the clumsiness and clambering of this world will be left behind in "love's unbreakable heaven" where our souls will float in eternal glory of . . . [here we go again] spilt bourbon (!). I just love the persona's wry sense of humor. His beloved doesn't just break vases, she shipwrecks them. Tough taxi drivers are terrified of her. Streetcars go apoplectic, and lipstick grins on coat collars. The poem itself is the "wry music" referenced in line 22, its wild rhythms and tongue-in-cheek humor sounding counterpoints to the genuine love being expressed. The gentle amusement keeps us from taking it all too seriously . . . until the final stanza.

In yet another unanticipated turn, the persona implores his darling never to leave him. Be early, be late, smash glasses, it does not matter. The final two lines create a momentary semantic confusion: "For should your hands drop. . . ." Well, these hands have been dropping lots of things right from the first line. Not until we reach the end of line 23 do we clearly realize that the persona means "drop" as in . . . well, drop dead, "white and empty." Here's yet another unexpected turn, the intrusion of death, suddenly, awkwardly. And if that sudden death should occur, then all the toys of the world would break. That's also momentarily confusing for us, but one slightly antiquated meaning of the word "toy" is "a small item of little monetary value, but treasured for some other special reason." So the persona may be saying that everything that he treasures—all the toys of his world—would shatter. What a breathtaking sentiment this then becomes. For all her clumsiness, the persona has placed his heart in her hands, knowing that in this one area, "people and love" she "moves at ease." Indeed, he imagines that the *only* thing that could cause her to drop his heart would be her death, and when she dies his heart will indeed break.

We can barely turn a page in the Bible without encountering imperfect human beings like the beloved of "Love Poem." Exodus offers us an early example: "Moses said to the Lord, 'Oh, my Lord, I am not eloquent, either heretofore or since thou hast spoken to thy servant; but I am slow of speech and tongue.' Then the Lord said to him, 'Who has made man's mouth? Who makes him dumb, or deaf, or seeing, or blind? Is it not I, the Lord? Now therefore go, and I will be with your mouth and teach you what you shall speak'" (4:10–12). God has a long and distinguished history of choosing deeply flawed people (as if there were any other kind) to do his work, and the beloved in this poem takes her place among them. I love the way the persona focuses on the hands of this woman—he adores them! Sure, these hands shipwreck vases and smash glasses, but the same clumsy hands also steady the stumbling drunk and reach out to welcome the uncertain refugee at the door. It almost seems as though God has said to her, "Go! I will be with your hands, and teach you what you should do." He will let none of us use our flaws as our excuses.

Advent Meditation 4
"Making the House Ready for the Lord"
by Mary Oliver

Dear Lord, I have swept and I have washed but
    still nothing is as shining as it should be
for you. Under the sink, for example, is an
    uproar of mice—it is the season of their
many children. What shall I do? And under the eaves   *line 5*
    and through the walls the squirrels
have gnawed their ragged entrances—but it is the season
    when they need shelter, so what shall I do? And
the raccoon limps into the kitchen and opens the cupboard
    while the dog snores, the cat hugs the pillow: *line 10*
what shall I do? Beautiful is the new snow falling
    in the yard and the fox who is staring boldly
up the path, to the door. And still I believe you will
    come, Lord: you will, when I speak to the fox,
the sparrow, the lost dog, the shivering sea-goose, know   *line 15*
    that really I am speaking to you whenever I say,
as I do all morning and afternoon: Come in, Come in.

I encourage you to read the poem several more times and work through the four steps outlined on page 12, or use the discussion questions about the poem on page 124.

The inner Martha: Luke tells us that Jesus entered a village one day, and "a woman named Martha received him into her house." Martha had a sister, Mary, "who sat at the Lord's feet and listened to his teaching. But Martha was distracted with much serving; and she went to him and said, 'Lord, do you not care that my sister has left me to serve alone? Tell her then to help me.' But the Lord answered her, 'Martha, Martha, you are anxious and troubled about many things; one thing is needful. Mary has chosen the good portion, which shall not be taken away from her'" (10:38–42). The first moment from the Bible I think of when I read "Making the House Ready for the Lord" is Jesus's response to Martha. Do not be anxious and distracted about matters that are not needful. What a great Advent message. Try to imagine this poem if the persona were to persevere in the initial thought expressed in that first sentence, sweeping and washing, shooing the mice out into the cold, patching those ragged entrances, taking the broom to the raccoon, all for the purpose of presenting a bright and shiningly perfect domicile to the Lord. The persona does, in fact, make the house ready for the Lord, not by a rigorous house-cleaning routine but by focusing on a central question in the poem: "What shall I do?"

The inner Paul: In Acts, chapter 22, Paul describes his conversion to Christianity: "As I made my journey and drew near to Damascus, about noon a great light from heaven suddenly shone about me. And I fell to the ground and heard a voice saying to me, 'Saul, Saul, why do you persecute me?' And I answered, 'Who are you, Lord?' And he said to me, 'I am Jesus of Nazareth whom you are persecuting.' . . . And I said, 'What shall I do, Lord?' And the Lord said to me, 'Rise, and go into Damascus, and there you will be told all that is appointed for you to do'" (6–10). The persona of "Making the House Ready for the Lord" asks, with Paul, what shall I do? And the answer comes back to the persona: abandon the mop and bucket, open the pantry door, pass out the pillows. Forget the spit and polish. Do you love me? Feed my sheep.

Structure: Mary Oliver exquisitely delineates a tension between fussy orderliness and charitable chaos within the very structure of the poem. Begging the readers' indulgence, below you will see the seventeen lines of "Making the House Ready for the Lord" as I think they would appear if the poet had wished to foreground the arrangement of repeated words on the page:

Dear <u>Lord</u>, I have swept and I have washed but <u>still</u> nothing is as
    shining as it should be for you.
Under the sink, for example, is an uproar of mice
—it is the season of their many children.
What shall I do?
And under the eaves and through the walls the squirrels
have gnawed their ragged entrances
—but it is the season when they need shelter,
so what shall I do?
And the raccoon limps into the kitchen and opens the cupboard
while the dog snores, the cat hugs the pillow:
what shall I do?

Beautiful is the new snow falling in the yard
and the fox who is staring boldly up the path, to the door.

And <u>still</u> I believe you will *come*, <u>Lord</u>: you will,
when I *speak* to the fox, the sparrow, the lost dog, the shivering
    sea-goose,
know that really I am *speaking* to you whenever I say,
as I do all morning and afternoon: *Come* in, Come in.

In this form, the linguistic patterns become perfectly clear. For instance,
we can easily perceive the repetition in lines 2 through 11 ("under," "it
is the season," and "what shall I do?"). We can also see much more
clearly the framing *chiasmus* of lines 1 and 14 (underlined above for
your convenience):

    A. Lord
        B. still nothing is as shining as it should be
        B. still I believe you will come
    A. Lord

This chiasmus supports what I see as just a touch of conversion in
"Making the House Ready for the Lord," a movement from Martha
to Mary, from Saul to Paul. The persona moves from anxiety that his

house is not ready to faith in the arrival of the Lord anyway. The foundation of this transformation is suggested by a second chiasmus embedded in the final four lines of this wonderful poem (italicized above for your convenience):

A. Come, Lord
    B. when I speak to the fox
    B. really I am speaking to you
A. Come in, come in.

By the poem's conclusion, the persona has become Mary, sitting at the feet of the Lord; he basks in the same bright light of the converted Paul. What is needful, Lord? What am I appointed to do? The poem reminds me so strongly of a passage from Matthew in which Jesus teaches the disciples that, in order to inherit the kingdom prepared for them, they must reach out to those in need. "[F]or I was hungry and you gave me food," Jesus says, "I was thirsty and you gave me drink, I was a stranger and you welcomed me, I was naked and you clothed me, I was sick and you visited me. . . . as you did it to one of the least of these my brethren, you did it to me" (25: 34–40). As the persona realizes by the end of the poem, when he is speaking to the fox, the lost dog, the shivering sea goose, he is actually speaking to the Lord. One of the most utterly charming dimensions of this poem, and one typical of this poet, is how it expands the definition of "my neighbor" to those in creation not necessarily human. Why should "the least of these" not include the stray dog, the hungry raccoon, or the fallen sparrow? When the persona provides shelter and food to these lost, these least, these powerless, when he welcomes them into his home, he invites God in as well. And thus the house is made ready.

Why not structure this poem, this prayer, so that all these beautiful patterns and repetitions would become more discernable? I think it is the poet's way of offering an ironic statement about the value of outward order. After all, if we look at the poem as Oliver has structured it, it seems perfectly balanced, with each line about the same length, as neatly stacked as folded towels in the linen closet. The poet has presented a work as "swept" and "washed" and "shining" as the persona wishes his house could be, yet both poet and persona ultimately recognize that the Lord does not require this type of readiness. Instead, he looks inside, through our ragged entrances, for love and charity. He peers through the holes in our walls. He checks under our sinks, looking for the uproar. Messy in here? A bit chaotic even? Done in my service? Well okay then. Let's pull up a chair.

A couple of final things: If you really want to get practically microscopic in thinking about the patterns in "Making the House Ready for the Lord," consider how often the sound/sight of that central question, "what shall I do," is reiterated in the poem. Not only do we see an unusually high number of words with double l's ("shall," "still," "walls," "falling," "will," "pillow," "really," "all," some of which are repeated several times), but also the vowel sound of "do" recurs with remarkable frequency. Take, for instance, line 11, with "shall" and "falling" bracketing the repeated vowel sound:

> what sha<u>ll</u> I d<u>o</u>? Be<u>au</u>tiful is the n<u>ew</u> snow fa<u>ll</u>ing.

Fold in repetitions of "y<u>ou</u> wi<u>ll</u>" near the poem's conclusion and the phrase "I d<u>o</u> a<u>ll</u>" in line 17, and I don't think it strains interpretation to suggest the entire poem echoes that Pauline question.

Finally, as we prepare to move from Advent to Christmas Eve, this seems an opportune moment to point out that all the poems we have read so far for Advent feature literal or metaphorical thresholds. The disappointed persona of "The Collar" threatens departure, poised at a metaphorical threshold in her life. The persona of Shakespeare's "Sonnet 29" finds herself ultimately singing hymns at the gates of heaven. The beloved of "Love Poem" (surely a kindred spirit to Oliver's persona) welcomes the uncertain refugee at the door. "Making the House Ready for the Lord" features "ragged entrances," a cupboard door, and the fox staring boldly at the main entrance of the house. As we celebrate Advent 4, we find ourselves poised on a threshold. The moment we have been anticipating draws near. The Eternal breaks through into mortality, opening the way for all who believe. Come, Lord Jesus. Come in. Come in.

CHRISTMAS EVE
"The Oxen" by Thomas Hardy
(December 24, 1915)

Christmas Eve, and twelve of the clock.
"Now they are all on their knees,"
An elder said as we sat in a flock
By the embers in hearthside ease.   *line 4*

We pictured the meek mild creatures where
They dwelt in their strawy pen,
Nor did it occur to one of us there
To doubt they were kneeling then.   *line 8*

So fair a fancy few would weave
In these years! Yet, I feel,
If someone said on Christmas Eve,
"Come; see the oxen kneel   *line 12*

In the lonely barton* by yonder coomb*
Our childhood used to know,"
I should go with him in the gloom,
Hoping it might be so.   *line 16*

barton: farmyard

coomb: small valley or hollow

I encourage you to read the poem several more times and work through the four steps outlined on page 12, or use the discussion questions about the poem on page 125.

Christmas Eve: A host of legends have sprung up about animals and Christmas Eve. Some say, for instance, that roosters crow at midnight in triumphant recognition of the Christ child. Shakespeare mentions this tradition in *Hamlet*, writing that "this bird of dawning singeth all night long." Others say that animals, especially horses, acquire the power of speech on Christmas Eve in order to sing hymns of praise and thanksgiving. And then there's the legend that Thomas Hardy references in this poem, that various barnyard animals (and, according to some, even wild animals like deer) kneel at midnight on Christmas Eve.

All of this is quite extraordinary considering that, other than sheep out in the fields, no animals are mentioned at all in Luke, the only New Testament account of that night. (Matthew also gives us a nativity narrative, but it focuses on the arrival of the wise men from the east after the birth of Jesus.) So, a couple of things before we turn to the poem itself: First, we have no way of knowing for certain that *any* animals were present at Jesus's birth. Yes, he was wrapped in swaddling clothes and laid in a manger (Luke mentions that detail several times), and given that location, we can reasonably assume that some barnyard creatures *may* have been present . . . but we don't know for sure. Second, in the context of this Biblical textual lack, why has this Christmas Eve bestiary emerged and endured?

Shakespeare, again, offers one possible answer. In *Hamlet*, a minor character named Marcellus, who speaks of the rooster-crowing legend, goes on to elaborate: "And then, they say, no [evil] spirit dare stir abroad, / The nights are wholesome, then no planets strike, / No fairy takes, nor witch hath power to charm, / So hallowed and so gracious is that time." Marcellus's speech suggests the legends may have come about partly as testimony to the holiness and sanctity of Christmas Eve. We might also recall that Christ came to redeem not just humankind, but all of creation, so for all of creation to mark the birth of the Savior seems entirely appropriate, if not mandatory. Mary Oliver has already suggested to us that creatures in need can be our neighbors, so why not imagine them kneeling in prayer? I recall that in Luke, chapter 19, some Pharisees chastise Jesus, telling him to silence his disciples, who are loudly praising God for the mighty works they have seen. Jesus responds: "I tell you, if these [people] were silent, the very stones would cry out" (40). In the context of singing stones, the idea of kneeling cattle or speaking horses doesn't seem so very farfetched. Its nonbiblical origin notwithstanding, Hardy has made great use of the legend in his brief, moving work on modernity and faith.

Structure: The poet has constructed a work of four equal stanzas, but upon completing a first read we can discern its further division into two equal parts. As we encounter lines 9 and 10 ("So fair a fancy few would weave / In these years!"), we realize that the first two *quatrains* represent a memory of faith traditions from the past. Until we reach those lines, though, we cannot be totally sure if the persona is recalling events that occurred many years ago or just last night. Note that the first two lines of the poem unfold in present tense and line 2 begins with "Now." Frankly, I love this touch, as it subtly suggests that this moment from years ago remains very much present for the persona and foreshadows the wistful longing more fully expressed in the final two lines. (Temporal ambiguity characterizes all four of the Christmas and Epiphany poems I have chosen for this volume, which seems entirely appropriate to me as poets contemplate a moment when the divine eternal breaks into human history.)

Note the effective realization of the faith community in those first eight lines. The "elder" of the group states his belief simply and straightforwardly to his "flock" seated at the hearth, an image that reminds me of a congregation gathered around an altar. This congregation appears unified in its beliefs, for not a single member thinks to question what the elder preaches. Doubt enters only at line 9, after we suddenly leap forward in time, and a shared article of faith from the past becomes a created, woven "fancy." The persona's pronoun use intensifies a contrast between community and self. In the first two stanzas, she twice uses "we" to refer to the Christmas Eve gathering. This pronoun completely disappears after that, replaced by first person singular. The long ago faith community with almost no individuation is reduced years later to an isolated persona struggling with the faith her "childhood used to know."

Persona: I find the attitude of the persona in the final eight lines one of the most interesting things in the poem. While she seems to dismiss the faith from years ago as a woven "fancy," she quickly alters direction in line 10. *Yet*, she says . . . *if*. Those two words prepare us for what follows, the persona's open-mindedness that this "fancy" just might be a truth. Unlike her childhood days, when doubt seemed literally unthinkable, in the present the persona imagines someone asking her to traipse over to the barton and check things out. And the persona says she would go, too, carrying her renunciation but also carrying her hope. I like to imagine her pausing at the threshold, wondering what she might see inside.

Some readers will disparage "The Oxen," written during World War I, as leaning too heavily on nostalgia. Especially in the era of mustard gas and trench warfare, the persona could be seen as longing for a simpler, more innocent time, a time when a group of people could be bound together by shared beliefs and traditions. This reading may have some validity, but I feel the poem offers more complexity than that. The persona finds the faith community of her childhood appealing, yet complacent. The "flock" of yesteryear seemed perfectly content to accept the teachings of the elder without interrogation. The mature persona, on the other hand, has embraced her doubt and yet stands prepared to have it tested by what she might find in a barn on Christmas Eve. I am reminded of a poem by Angelus Silesius which reads, quite simply, "If you could turn your heart / into a cowstall, / Christ would be born again on earth!" Does the persona long for this? To turn her heart into a cowstall? Is this poem a prayer for something latent inside of her (the idea of eternity?) to be reawakened?

Come, let us adore him: When we hear the word "Come" on Christmas Eve, we expect a call to worship the Christ Child. And indeed that word in line 12 amounts to an altar call. The persona is invited, along with shepherds in the field and wise men from the east, to come and witness this birth. The placing of Christ in a manger (from the French verb "to eat") as worshippers gather around him has long been seen as a foreshadowing of the Eucharistic Table. The persona, with all of her modern skepticism and doubt, seems willing to respond to this call, hoping to see something that will restore her belief. What modern reader does not relate to this doubt, this hope? All faith is an irrational leap. Changing water into wine? Raising the dead? Resurrection? How can we possibly believe in these incredible things? Even the twelve disciples, who knew and loved Jesus and witnessed what he did, often struggled to understand and to believe. The New Testament offers endless examples suggesting that faith brings not serenity. "I believe!" cries the father in Mark 9. "Help my unbelief!" "The Oxen" poses a legitimate question: whose faith is stronger, the elder who, never thinking to doubt, remains "in hearthside ease," or the persona, alienated from her own spirituality, who yet would willingly venture with her friend into the gloom? What is Advent if not a journey through the deepening twilight, hoping against hope for a glimpse of the light?

In a piece I wrote called *The Apostles*, I have Peter say this about Doubting Thomas: "Frankly, none of us ever really doubted Thomas' faith. In the days following Jesus's death, we were all afraid and confused. It really isn't fair that history remembers him, and him alone, as 'Doubting Thomas.'" According to the Gospel of John, when Thomas hears the news about the resurrection, he declares: "Unless I see in his hands the wound made by the nails and put my finger into the wound, and put my hand into his side, I will never believe" (20:25, Weymouth New Testament). "Because you have seen me," Jesus tells him during their encounter afterward, "you have believed. Blessed are those who have not seen and yet have believed" (John 20:29, Weymouth New Testament). We, like the persona in "The Oxen," are those who have not seen. We have not seen the miracle in Cana. We have not seen the empty tomb. We have not seen the spear wound in the side of the risen Lord. We have not seen the oxen kneel at midnight.

So we could say we have some grounds for our modern skepticism. *Yet . . . if . . .* we were called to prepare a meal for a sick friend, how joyfully would we do so? How do we respond in the face of a homeless veteran's empty cup? When invited to join a church group to make a prison visit, do we go? We might be hard pressed to find a local barton, yet we have our share of opportunities to step into the gloom. Have we the courage of Hardy's persona, unsure what we might find there, yet knowing we could see in one of these faces the light of Christmas Eve . . . and hoping it might be so?

CHRISTMAS
"Bezhetsk" by Anna Akhmatova
(December 26, 1921)

There are white churches there, and the crackle of icicles,
The cornflower eyes of my son are blossoming there.
Diamond nights above the ancient town, and yellower
Than lime-blossom honey is the moon's sickle.   *line 4*
From plains beyond the river dry snow-storms fly in,
And the people, like the angels in the fields, rejoice.
They have tidied the best room, lit in the icon case
The tiny lamps. On an oak table the Book is lying.   *line 8*
There stern memory, so ungiving now,
Threw open her doors to me, with a low bow;
But I did not enter, and I slammed the fearful door;
And the town rang with the news of the child that was born. *line 12*

*I encourage you to read the poem several more times and work through the
four steps outlined on page 12, or you can use the discussion questions about
the poem on page 126.*

Memory: What holiday evokes more memories than Christmas? Even
for non-Christians, the season abounds with candlelit traditions and
tables laden with favorite foods, some prepared only this one time
of the year. Many, like the persona of "The Oxen," recall gatherings
with family and friends or celebrations featuring the exchange of gifts.
Others, though, may find themselves overwhelmed with sadness and
depression, focusing on what they lack in the presence of so much
abundance. The lonely or impoverished can feel excluded from the

massive celebration they witness unfolding around them. Those whose memories of the holidays are less than perfect may feel that they have been singularly deprived of the seemingly universal childhood wonder of the season. Anna Akhmatova captures this tension between the cultural celebration in a small town and memories so disturbing that the persona feels he must slam the door on them, never to return.

Where and when: The title of the poem suggests the significance of location, and the repetition of "there" in lines 1, 2, and 9 strengthens that suggestion. The persona's memories are tied to a very specific time and place. The first line places us immediately within a winter season ("icicles"), but we don't understand until line 6, with its reference to angels rejoicing in the fields, that the persona's mind is settled specifically in late December. With this knowledge, our second reading, especially of the first six lines, will differ from the first. In the context of Christmas, the reference to white churches carries different significance, and the blossoming "cornflower eyes of my son" now seems a possible foreshadowing of the birth of Jesus Christ (the repetition of the word "blossom" suggesting the familiar yuletide image of the rose that blooms midwinter). Recalling "Diamond nights above the ancient town" stirs the persona's specific memories of Bezhetsk, yet we could also imagine stars above the town of Bethlehem. I cannot help but wonder if the poet has chosen this particular place name because of its similarity to **Beth**le**hem**, a thought which, again, emphasizes the importance of location.

Who is the persona? The persona, now an adult with a child, reveals an intimate recollection of this town and its customs, suggesting a long period of residence or childhood upbringing. He recalls physical environs (the buildings, the cold, the night sky with its stars and moon) as well as holiday traditions (tidying the best room as if for a guest, lighting lamps in the icon case, and the church bells ringing in celebration). I feel a palpable sense of longing in warm memories of lit candles and polished oak, and yet the most intriguing moment of the poem begins with the phrase evoking "stern memory." At some point in the past, memory "threw open her doors" to the persona (intriguing image), bowing low as if to welcome him in. But the persona refuses to cross that threshold (another threshold!), instead slamming that "fearful door" closed again. The lines engender a question for which the poem offers no clear answer: among the warm holiday recollections, what unendurable memories lurk behind that fearful door?

A little background provides some insight: Born in 1889, Anna Akhmatova grew up in a small town (Tsarskoye Selo) near St. Petersburg. Widely praised in her country through the early nineteenth century, Akhmatova fell into disfavor after the Russian Revolution. Soviet secret police executed her first husband, and her son remained a political prisoner for many years. Her work was officially censored under Stalin, though she never stopped writing and never gave in to the temptation to leave her homeland. Much of her poetry deals with loss and the difficulty of artistic expression in a repressive society. In this context, we should note that Bezhetsk really exists, a town north of Moscow, and its oldest structure is a white bell tower built in the late seventeenth century. The church associated with the bell tower has disappeared, destroyed during the atheistic Soviet era.

This personal and historical background cannot (and should not) provide clear definitive answers to the questions raised by "Bezhetsk." While we still cannot say for certain what memories the persona refuses to face, specific knowledge relevant to the title of the poem raises some distinct possibilities we might otherwise not consider: A Soviet takeover of the village? The destruction of the church and by extension a way of life gone forever? Domestic terrorism? Persecution? I must say, I find it fascinating that the persona recalls, in this translation at least, the moon in the shape of a yellow "sickle" (a term *foreshadowed* in line 1 by the phonetically similar "icicles," the crackle of which seems a bit more ominous in retrospect). This familiar harvesting instrument served from early in the twentieth century as half of the hammer-and-sickle symbol for communism. Its appearance in this poem, suggestive if not definitive, perhaps provides a subtle clue to the nature of the persona's fearful memories.

Faith during a time of trial: In his second letter to the Corinthians, Paul writes of the difficulty of maintaining faith during a time of trial: "we have this treasure in earthen vessels, to show that the transcendent power belongs to God and not to us. We are afflicted in every way, but not crushed; perplexed, but not driven to despair; persecuted, but not forsaken; struck down, but not destroyed" (4:7–9). Akhmatova's "Bezhetsk" expresses loss, what the village has lost and what the persona has lost, yet the poem also participates in the paradox articulated by Paul. The persona describes memory as "stern" and "ungiving," yet also vividly and warmly recalls a moon in a star-studded sky and candlelight (the words "yellower," "honey," "lamps," and "oak" cast a subtle golden sheen over some of these recollections). What shall we make of this? What does the slamming of this door mean? On which side of a threshold does the persona stubbornly hold his ground? Does he remain outside, with the community rejoicing, or inside, alone with his pain? Has he found his faith? Or lost it?

Paul goes on in the same epistle to explain that we carry within us the death *and* the life of Jesus. We must embrace both the darkness *and* the light. In that context, I note an interesting use of "and" in Akhmatova's poem. For instance, in lines 5 and 6, the persona tells us that from beyond the river dry snow-storms fly in, *and* (not *but*) the people rejoice. At the poem's conclusion, he says "I slammed the fearful door; / *And* the town rang with the news of the child that was born." In both cases, the people celebrate not in spite of the storms and fear, but in addition to (or maybe, perhaps, because of?). The final line, written in past tense, may suggest a holiday observance that no longer exists, a past that the persona can never reclaim. There is a danger here, a lure of nostalgia, mourning too much for things gone by. As I have progressed in my treatments through surgery and radiation and on to other therapies, I have learned the difficult lesson of dwelling in the past, of grieving overmuch for the precancerous life I can never reclaim. I have learned that memory can be warm and sustaining, but also ungenerous, even agonizing. Regret makes a dangerous enemy, and some doors are best left unopened. Still, let us not overlook that the poem portrays joy in its final image, and its last word, "born," anticipates hope and new life. In deep midwinter, does the persona remember the blossoms? In the presence of the Christ Child, can he find the strength to persevere? Anna Kamienska has written that we must learn to pray through love and the magic of a winter snowfall, and also through the tears that do not end. While I am not afflicted with endless tears, I do feel these days more acutely than ever the fragility of my own "earthen vessel" and must frequently remind myself that in the midst of my perplexed struggle I am never forsaken. In an image taken from this wonderfully complex poem, threatening storms fly in from the plains, *and* the people of the town, like the angels in the fields, rejoice.

EPIPHANY I

"Journey of the Magi" by T.S. Eliot (1927)

'A cold coming we had of it,
Just the worst time of the year
For a journey, and such a long journey:
The ways deep and the weather sharp,
The very dead of winter.'   *line 5*
And the camels galled, sore-footed, refractory,
Lying down in the melting snow.
There were times we regretted
The summer palaces on slopes, the terraces,
And the silken girls bringing sherbet.   *line 10*
Then the camel men cursing and grumbling
And running away, and wanting their liquor and women,
And the night-fires going out, and the lack of shelters,
And the cities hostile and the towns unfriendly
And the villages dirty and charging high prices: *line 15*
A hard time we had of it.
At the end we preferred to travel all night,
Sleeping in snatches,
With the voices singing in our ears, saying
That this was all folly.   *line 20*

Then at dawn we came down to a temperate valley,
Wet, below the snow line, smelling of vegetation;
With a running stream and a water-mill beating the darkness,
And three trees on the low sky,
And an old white horse galloped away in the meadow. *line 25*

Then we came to a tavern with vine-leaves over the lintel,
Six hands at an open door dicing for pieces of silver,
And feet kicking the empty wine-skins,
But there was no information, and so we continued
And arrived at evening, not a moment too soon   *line 30*
Finding the place; it was (you may say) satisfactory.

All this was a long time ago, I remember,
And I would do it again, but set down
This set down
This: were we led all that way for   *line 35*
Birth or Death? There was a Birth, certainly,
We had evidence and no doubt. I had seen birth and death,
But had thought they were different; this Birth was
Hard and bitter agony for us, like Death, our death,
We returned to our places, these Kingdoms,   *line 40*
But no longer at ease here, in the old dispensation,
With an alien people clutching their gods.
I should be glad of another death.

I encourage you to read the poem several more times and work through the four steps outlined on page 12, or use the discussion questions about the poem on page 127.

Because of the biblical and historical insistence that the Three Wise Men were male, I am characterizing the persona of this poem as masculine.

We have seen his star in the East, and have come to worship him. . . . When they saw the star, they rejoiced exceedingly with great joy; and going into the house they saw the child with Mary his mother, and they fell down and worshiped him. (Matthew 2:2, 10–11)

Persona: Eliot based the first five lines of "Journey of the Magi" on two sentences from a sermon the Reverend Lancelot Andrewes delivered in London on December 25, 1622: "A cold coming they had of it at this time of the year, just the worst time of the year to take a journey, and specially a long journey. The ways deep, the weather sharp, the days short, the sun farthest off, *in solstitio brumaldi*, the very dead of the winter." Andrewes's sermon continues, ". . . And these difficulties they overcame, of a wearisome, irksome, troublesome, dangerous, unseasonable journey; and for all this they came. And came cheerfully and quickly . . . made all this haste that they might be there to worship Him with all the possible speed they could. Sorry for nothing so much as that they could not be there soon enough, with the very first, to do it even this day, the day of His birth."

Andrewes's words, not to mention the familiar verses from Matthew, chapter 2, lead us to anticipate Magi rushing to the manger filled with hope and joy, even exultation. They have seen a star, they know what it means, and they have deliberately set out to find a newborn king whom they fully intend to worship. With all this in mind, what a shock we experience to encounter this crabby old man of Eliot's poem, kvetching about the cold and the camels and the many difficulties of traveling, especially in winter. The voices ringing in their ears sing not *Glory to God in the highest*, but rather *the three of you are fools*. Our expectations, like the persona's in the final stanza, have been upended. He thought he knew what "birth" was and what "death" was; it turns out he was wrong. Chances are, so are we.

The persona probably thinks he knows what "winter" is as well, and "summer," and "spring," yet time and the seasons seem oddly muddled in "Journey of the Magi," as they were in "The Oxen" and "Bezhetsk."[1] While the magus clearly establishes the time of the journey as "the very dead of winter," two lines later he describes his camels as lying down in the melting snow (suggesting a spring thaw?), and his regretful recollections of what he has left behind (palaces with open terraces and silken girls delivering sherbet) generate a summery warmth. This seasonal slipperiness is emphasized in lines 21–23 as the persona describes their descent from the mountains in terms that clearly suggest the movement of winter into spring: a temperate climate, smells of vegetation, and an ice-free, running stream. In the context of a water-mill "beating the darkness," surely it is no accident that this descent takes place at

---

1. I note with interest that the speakers of three consecutive poems live in the shadow of memory. Ahkmatova's persona slams the door on fearful recollections. Hardy's speaker contrasts Christmas Eve memories with her current faith experiences. His life-shattering journey haunts Eliot's wise man for the rest of his days.

dawn, that *liminal* time of day as darkness recedes and light ascends. The poem captures events in a state of flux.

Birth and Death: The middle section of the poem intrigues with its multiple biblical *allusions*. Some are fairly obvious: "three trees on the low sky" suggests Golgotha, and "pieces of silver" reminds me of Judas and his betrayal. "Six hands . . . dicing" seems more obscure, but in context may cause some readers to think of Roman soldiers at the foot of the cross casting lots for Christ's garments. A description of "a tavern with vine-leaves over the lintel" may puzzle at first, but if we follow a chain of logic that allows us to read "vine-leaves" as a reference to wine and wine as symbolic of blood, then we might see this image as an oblique reference to the blood of the Passover and a reminder that Christ, about to be born, will become the Passover Lamb for all. Fascinating. In the midst of a journey to witness the birth of Jesus, we observe, along with the Magi, so many details that fore-shadow his death.

In that context, especially in a poem where winter and spring seem to exist simultaneously (again I think of the rose that blooms midwinter), the poet has prepared us well for what may be the most intriguing lines of the poem: "I had seen birth and death / But had thought they were different." At the birth of Christ, this persona does not celebrate, he mourns: "this Birth was / Hard and bitter agony for us, like death, our death." After a few moments with this new king, the magi return to their places, but they know nothing will ever be the same. They perceive that the old dispensation will pass away (indeed, has already passed away) and that their very own people (and the old gods they desperately clutch) have become alien to them now that they have worshipped in the presence of Eternity.

Old horse, old wine: Of all the lines in the poem, this one I found the most confusing: "And an old white horse galloped away in the meadow." Upon first readings, I could not for the life of me figure out what this might mean. Some research, however, turned up a wonderful possibility: The White Horse of Uffington. I had never heard of this. The White Horse of Uffington, a 300-foot-long hill figure formed by trenches dug in the ground and filled with white chalk, is comparable in design to other horses in Celtic art and on Celtic coins. The horse could be as old as 1000 BC or as recent as 100 AD, but among those who have studied the artifact, the general consensus is that it predates Jesus Christ. In the context of the poem, with its passing away of old regimes, it seems to me that we could interpret "an old white horse [galloping] away in the meadow" as the passing of old, pagan cultures in the face of a new millennium.

When we think of Jesus, we often think of wine. For his first miracle, he transformed water into wine, and the wine he serves to his disciples on Maundy Thursday he calls his blood, an event we commemorate at every Eucharist. In this verse from Luke, Jesus describes his presence and teachings as new wine. With his coming, all old wineskins must be discarded: "no one puts new wine into old wineskins; if he does, the new wine will burst the skins and it will be spilled, and the skins will be destroyed. But new wine must be put into fresh wineskins" (Luke 5:37–38). In a poem that mentions the passing of an "old dispensation," it is surely no coincidence that we see feet kicking old, empty, discarded wineskins on the floor of the tavern. New wine must go into new wineskins.

New Testament writings relentlessly associate Jesus with the new. "Behold!" says the figure on the throne in Revelation, "I make all things new" (21:5). Paul writes in 2 Corinthians that in Christ "the new has come." But if the new has come, the old must pass away, or be transformed (in this context, we can imagine the Revelation figure of Jesus on a white horse as transforming the pagan image of the White Horse of Uffington). For those associated with "the old," this passage can be a "Hard and bitter agony," and by the poem's conclusion, the persona says he should be glad of another death. His own? If so, then grief and despair sound the final note of this "journey." But in this work (where birth is death and death, birth), need we necessarily conclude that the magus, after years of alienation and suffering, just wants to die? Might his many oblique references to the crucifixion reveal instead a deep desire for the death of Christ and the hope for salvation that it brings? He does, after all, declare that he would make the trip again (though his tone leaves the possibility of insincerity wide open). Why make this admission unless he knows on some level that for all the inconvenience and cold, for all the bitter agony and the passing of his very way of life, returning to embrace this birth (this death) represents his only hope for the eternity he was surely searching for from the very beginning? Is this poem not a prayer, a request to finish a journey he began so very many years ago?

Let's face it: as we all rush to the manger to see the newborn King, we cannot help but also hasten, simultaneously, to the cross. We witness God's ultimate expression of eternity, his son, and our imaginations leap forward to the day when the gates will fall and our way back into this infinite light will be made free and clear. I believe that this extraordinary persona, as he gazed upon the infant Jesus, understood exactly what he saw: The message in the bottle. The Epiphany. The moment in time that abides forever and gives without ceasing. "Journey of the Magi" reminds me so vividly of the verse from *We Three Kings* in which an ointment of myrrh is offered to the Christ child:

> *Myrrh is mine, its bitter perfume*
> *Breathes a life of gathering gloom;*
> *Sorrowing, sighing, bleeding, dying,*
> *Sealed in the stone cold tomb.*

The Jews used perfumed ointments of myrrh in their funeral preparations, and we recall that Nicodemus brought "a mixture of myrrh and aloes, about a hundred pounds' weight" to prepare Jesus's body for burial (John 19:39). Unto to us has been born a savior, but even as we celebrate his birth, our fallen selves long for another death. This babe can be no savior without what lies ahead: the hard and bitter agony of Golgotha and the terror of a stone cold tomb.

EPIPHANY 2

"Such Singing in the Wild Branches"
by Mary Oliver (2003)

It was spring
and finally I heard him
among the first leaves—
then I saw him clutching the limb   *line 4*

in an island of shade
with his red-brown feathers
all trim and neat for the new year.
First, I stood still   *line 8*

and thought of nothing.
Then I began to listen.
Then I was filled with gladness—
and that's when it happened,   *line 12*

when I seemed to float,
to be, myself, a wing or a tree—
and I began to understand
what the bird was saying,   *line 16*

and the sands in the glass
stopped
for a pure white moment
while gravity sprinkled upward   *line 20*

like rain, rising,
and in fact
it became difficult to tell just what it was that was singing—
it was the thrush for sure, but it seemed

not a single thrush, but himself, and all his brothers,
and also the trees around them,
as well as the gliding, long-tailed clouds
in the perfectly blue sky—all, all of them   *line 28*

were singing.
And, of course, yes, so it seemed,
so was I.
Such soft and solemn and perfect music doesn't last

for more than a few moments.
It's one of those magical places wise people
like to talk about.
One of the things they say about it, that is true,   *line 36*

is that, once you've been there,
you're there forever.
Listen, everyone has a chance.
Is it spring, is it morning?   *line 40*

Are there trees near you,
and does your own soul need comforting?
Quick, then—open the door and fly on your heavy feet; the song
may already be drifting away.

You will find the discussion questions for this poem on page 129.

Moses climbed a mountain to converse with God: He returned with
a covenant written in stone and a face gloriously aglow with the Holy
Spirit. The rest of the Israelites cowered in their tents. Sadly, over time
his facial splendor began to fade; so much so, in fact, that he placed a

veil over his visage to hide from the others the ebbing of this reflected power. This metaphorical veil of fear and deception continued to lie between the Israelites and God, a veil torn only at the death of Christ. Now, as much as we may *think* we would wish to stay on the mountaintop in the continuous presence of Almighty God, Paul writes that we are not like Moses. Fortunately, we are also not like those other Israelites. We get more than a mediated godhead, more than laws written in stone, more than fading splendor hidden behind a veil. We get a Christ, made Man, in us. The fleeting mountaintop experience becomes a moment that dwells within us forever, if we will let it. That is the subject of Mary Oliver's poem.

Join in with the singing: The persona of "Such singing in the wild branches" experiences such a fascinating journey. At the outset, clearly, this persona has been watching and listening. He has been waiting for a moment when finally he will hear a voice. Like T.S. Eliot's wise man, he has, in fact, been seeking eternity. Finally, the persona catches a whisper of song among the first leaves. He stands motionless. He empties his mind. He listens. He's filled with joy. And then comes this literally extra-ordinary moment when the persona seems to float, gravity itself suspended, sprinkling upward like rain rising, an evaporation image relevantly suggesting a transformation from the material to the spiritual. The persona seems to merge with the tree, or the thrush, and all creation seems to meld, all creation begins to sing. The thrush and all "his brothers" sing, yes, but also all the trees and even the clouds (that risen rain). To his astonishment, the persona discovers that he can *understand* the song, and thus can also sing along. Creation unifies and rises, singing, in a moment the persona declares will be with him forever, a moment in time that becomes material, a "magical place." But the poem does not end there. The persona next exhorts others to share this experience. "Listen," he says, "everyone has a chance." In lines bursting with *liminal* imagery, the persona encourages his listeners, if it is spring and it is morning, to open their doors, fly across their thresholds, find the trees and join in with the singing.

Dazed humility: So much can be said about this remarkable poem. The poet carefully prepares us for an experience of transformation and renewal by the first several lines, through which we learn that the season is spring, the beginning of a new cycle, and the trees are putting forth their first leaves—a time of rebirth. I also love the sort of dazed humility with which the persona recalls the experience. He *seemed* to float; it *seemed* as if the trees and clouds themselves were singing; it *seemed* as if he were singing too. This hesitance is complemented by a certain verbal stumbling here and there. Take this sequence, for instance, lines 23–24: "just what it was that was singing— / it was. . . ." We might dismiss this repetition of "was" as an amateurish compositional flaw if we could not recognize it instead as the humble groping for words by a persona trying to describe his experience. We see it again in lines 36–37, "that is true, / is that" a *chiasmic* construction that suggests a working into the center (the truth) which then reverses or changes what has come before ("that is" becomes "is that"). As we will see below, this chiasmic phrase works in harmony with the overall transformational nature of the entire poem.

Contingent and Absolute: In his second letter to the Corinthians, Paul writes: "Since we have such a hope, we are very bold, not like Moses, who put a veil over his face so that the Israelites might not see the end of the fading splendor. . . . to this day, when they read the old covenant, that same veil remains unlifted, because only through Christ is it taken away. . . . when a man turns to the Lord the veil is removed. . . . and we all, with unveiled face, beholding the glory of the Lord, are being changed into his likeness from one degree of glory to another" (3:13–18). Having experienced his own lightning bolt on the road to Damascus, Paul of all people knew from epiphanies. Glorious transformation lies at the heart of Oliver's poem. Gravity literally materializes, and rain becomes ethereal vapor, both reversing their direction. The movement of the poem remains relentlessly vertical. The eyes of the poet rise to heaven, searching for the thrush at the beginning of the poem and later continuing upward to the "gliding, long-tailed clouds," floating like kites "in the perfectly blue sky." Gravity sprinkles upward, rain rises, the persona floats. The sands in the hourglass, described in the only line of the poem composed of a single word, have "stopped." This word suspends the momentum of the poem just as the forward motion of time itself pauses for "a pure white moment" in which the persona will live for the rest of his life, and beyond: "once you've been there / you're there forever." The finite and the infinite converge as a fleeting moment becomes eternity—*once* becomes *forever*.[1] One degree of glory exchanged for another.

A final thought—the importance of listening: The singing is central to the poem, of course, but the persona could not participate in the music before stillness and emptiness and silence. Further, at the poem's conclusion he encourages others to listen as well, to go and hear the song it seems all creation sings in unison. I hear in this poem an echo of the Palm Sunday reading, which I also referenced earlier while discussing "The Oxen": some of the Pharisees have commanded Jesus to rebuke his disciples, to whom he replies, "I tell you, if these [people] were silent, the very stones would cry out." Finally, I note that the persona is not without a wry sense of humor; at lines 34–35, he describes his experience as "one of those magical places wise people / like to talk about." I perceive a bit of tongue-in-cheek here. Wise people may enjoy intellectualizing these moments, but as the persona asserts in line 39, "everyone has a chance." The mountain-top experience, or even just the peace and balm provided by a retreat into the woods, is not restricted to the smart people who bandy about words like "epiphany" and "transcendent." Everyone has access to this *forever* in the *once*. Is your heart heavy? Does your soul need comforting? Go. Listen.

---

1. Off topic from poetry, but much of the great literature I've read recently has precisely this as its theme: finding the infinite within the iron finitude of our lives. This from *The Fault in Our Stars*: "You gave me a forever within the numbered days, and I'm grateful" (260). And this from *The Elegance of the Hedgehog*: "Because from now on, for you, I'll be searching for those moments of always within never" (325). I urgently recommend both books to you.

LENT

IN ADVENT, WE BEGIN IN PENITENCE AND ASCEND rather quickly to the joy of Christmas.

In Lent, we again begin in penitence, but our road takes a longer, murkier path, downward, through excruciating pain and death. The light has arrived. Now will it endure? Ultimately we emerge from the terrifying chrysalis of a sealed tomb into new life, but first we must walk with temptation, fear, arrogance, suffering, betrayal, bitterness, and loss.

So the poetry in this section, especially as we near Good Friday, descends into a darkening twilight. But the poets do not despair. Rather, several of these Lent and Holy Week poems have touched me the most deeply at this time in my life. "A prayer that will be answered," "The Scattered Congregation," and "Heron Rises from the Dark, Summer Pond" have given me the courage to persevere through painful physical challenges and difficult emotional setbacks in hope of better days to come. The journey through dusk and darkness ends, we pray, with a sunrise.

If in Advent we wait for Eternity to come to us, through Lent we hope that Eternity will take us back with him. Advent makes the promise that Easter keeps.

ASH WEDNESDAY

"Ozymandias"
by Percy Bysshe Shelley (1818)

I met a traveller from an antique land
Who said: "Two vast and trunkless legs of stone
Stand in the desert. Near them, on the sand,
Half sunk, a shattered visage lies, whose frown,   *line 4*
And wrinkled lip, and sneer of cold command,
Tell that its sculptor well those passions read
Which yet survive, stamped on these lifeless things,
The hand that mocked them and the heart that fed.   *line 8*
And on the pedestal these words appear—
"My name is Ozymandias, king of kings:
Look on my works, ye Mighty, and despair!"
Nothing beside remains. Round the decay   *line 12*
Of that colossal wreck, boundless and bare,
The lone and level sands stretch far away.

You will find the discussion questions for this poem on page 130.

You will find the discussion questions for this poem on page 130.

Ramesses the Great: One of the many things I love about this poem is that, not unlike scripture itself, it brilliantly combines an ancient specificity with a modern relevance. Ozymandias, the Greek name for Ramesses II (also known as Ramesses the Great), was an Egyptian pharaoh who ruled from 1279 to 1213 BC. A builder, Ramesses particularly enjoyed erecting enormous statues of himself. According to the ancient Greek historian Diodurus Siculus, one of the largest statues in ancient Egypt had this as its inscription: "I am Ozymandias, king of kings; if anyone wishes to know what I am and where I lie, let him surpass me in some of my exploits." In fact, at about the same time that Percy Bysshe Shelley was working on this poem, a huge, seven-ton bust of Ramesses had been discovered and removed from Thebes by an archeologist named Giovanni Belzoni. This mammoth fragment would eventually arrive in London in 1821. Clearly, "Ozymandias" is thoroughly grounded in historical fact—a real pharaoh, actual statues, and an apparently authentic inscription, all of which serve as wonderfully apt metaphors for the mutability of everything in creation, no matter how powerful or colossally substantial. "Vanity of vanities," cries the Teacher, "all is vanity!"

This perfect Ash Wednesday poem offers its reader multiple images of disintegration and deterioration: two trunkless legs of stone stand in the sand; a shattered visage lies half sunk nearby; and later the remains of the statue are described as colossal wreckage. An ancient voice commands the observer to "Look on my works . . . and despair," yet nothing else remains to gaze upon but lonely and level sand as far as the eye can see. Ramesses has clearly missed the memo from the Teacher of Ecclesiastes: "For of the wise man as of the fool there is no enduring remembrance, seeing that in the days to come all will have been long forgotten" (2:16). The vaulting verticality of huge statues and mighty temples has been utterly flattened by the ravages of time and fate.

Sound and structure: Note how the sound and structure of the poem participate in its images and meanings. The very language creates a net of interwoven sound through *alliteration, consonance,* and *internal rhyme.* For instance, several word pairs linked by alliteration foreshadow and echo the central alliterative phrase of the poem ("**k**ing of **k**ings"): "**st**one" / "**st**and"; "**c**old" / "**c**ommand"; "**h**and" / "**h**eart"; "**m**y" / "**M**ighty"; "**b**oundless and **b**are"; and "**l**one and **l**evel." I am also intrigued to see how many words rhyme with the third syllable of Ozy**mand**ias: "land," "stand," "sand," "hand," and "command." The entire poem echoes its own title.[1] While the sounds of the poetry focus

---

1. By a wonderful linguistic coincidence, the third syllable of Ozy**mand**ias is identical to the first syllable of the Latin root *mandatum*, from which we get pharaoh-appropriate words like *demand, mandate,* and *command.* By an equally wonderful Lenten coincidence, this same Latin root gives us Maundy Thursday, that phrase referencing the "new commandment" Jesus gave his disciples after washing their feet the night of the Last Supper.

our auditory attention on boastful line 10 ("My name is Ozymandias, king of kings"), the structure of the poem participates in the decay that cuts the legs out from under this vaunting pedestal boasting. The poem is a *sonnet*, and as such, we would expect of it a regular structure and rhyme pattern. The first *quatrain* fulfills this expectation with its regular *abab* end-rhymed structure ("land," "stone," "sand," and "frown," though the *b*-rhyme is not quite perfect); however, the second *quatrain* offers an *acdc* pattern, most unexpected, and by the time we reach the final *sestet* (after the turn at line 9 which begins to focus our attention on the inscription), we encounter the irregular *edefef*. I think it's fair to assert that the poet intends this breakdown of traditional rhyme pattern as a deliberate, albeit rather subtle, disintegration of sonnet structure. The poem's form participates in creating its meaning.

Those passions which yet survive: In his essay "On Life," Shelley wrote that man has "a spirit within him at enmity with dissolution and nothingness." Again I recall Ecclesiastes and the idea of eternity placed within the human heart. Ozymandias has fought his war with time, and lost it. That which he constructed has dissolved, a sobering note, perhaps, for those poets who assure us that their words will last forever. Yet I feel like there's more going on here than just a reminder that things fall apart. The poem's emotional impact is carried, at least in part, by the contrast between the passions of antiquity and the rather dispassionate attitude of the persona. For, while the Ozymandias depicted in the stone remnants and inscription seems proud, arrogant, and condescending, the persona maintains an emotionally distant, neutral stance. Note for instance the unusual opening of the poem: "I met a traveller from an antique land / Who said. . . ." After these first ten words, the rest of the sonnet consists of the persona's quotation of a different speaker, the traveller, not the direct voice of the persona at all. Thus, the reader encounters, essentially, a second-hand description, the persona's recollection of what the traveller has related to him. This traveller has come from a faraway, "antique" land, so we anticipate that what follows might be remote, both physically and temporally (the classic "long ago and far away"), a removedness consistent with the narrative distance established in the first two lines. While we see powerful passions portrayed in the poem, the persona has not invited us to engage them, much less participate in them; rather, we are encouraged to hold the entire description at arm's length, to step back and judge dispassionately and rationally. The persona offers no judgment of her own, no "moral of the story," but instead allows the irony of the final five lines to speak for itself.

I do not mean to argue that "Ozymandias" doesn't pack a forceful punch, quite the contrary. The restraint renders the poem's impact all the more powerful. I believe that the emotional effect stems at least in part from the breathtakingly sudden reversal we witness late in the poem. Note the slow buildup of fiery qualities beginning with line 4. We see the shattered visage with its disdainful frown, then its arrogant sneer of cold command. A couple of lines later the pedestal inscription reveals the vaulting pride and literally monumental egotism of Ozymandias: "Look on my works, ye Mighty, and despair!" But observe what happens in line 12. Three potent words followed by a strong *caesura* nullify almost instantaneously this proud and arrogant boasting: "Nothing beside remains." Thud. With half a line all the mighty works, the statues, the temples, the palaces, and the crowns are reduced to a decayed colossus. All the lust for political power, all ego, all ambition, (passions, the poem assures us, "which yet survive") all devastatingly rendered a boundless nothingness. Vast expanses of level, wind-blown desert sand, stretching to the horizon in all directions, surround this bleak oasis, the isolated *remains* (well-chosen word there) of a once-triumphant monument to human achievement. The poet renders the image all the more stunning by the speed with which the narrative pulls the rug out from under us. We too experience a kind of psychological fall as we move with a heartbeat from "king of kings!" to "Nothing." Lines 10–12 of this poem may represent the most powerfully compressed representation in western literature of "pride goeth before a fall."

To dust we shall return: Obviously, I feel that "Ozymandias" offers a meditation on the folly of arrogance and pride. Like the persona of Shakespeare's "Sonnet 29," Ozymandias is nailed back into himself, his material wealth and power serving merely to promote self and diminish others to despair. As I pondered a more spiritual understanding of the poem, I turned to the apocryphal book of Sirach, which tells us that "Arrogance is hateful before the Lord and before men." In the same chapter, the author goes on to ask, "How can he who is dust and ashes be proud? For even in life his bowels decay. A long illness baffles the physician; the king of today will die tomorrow" (10:7, 9–10). Honestly, could there be a better verse to place next to this poem? For that matter, could there be a better verse for Ash Wednesday? Ultimately, it is not enough just to remember that we are dust and to dust we shall return; we must also remember *why* we must remember.

Our family purchases milk produced by a local dairy and sold in glass bottles. Not only do I love supporting the local economy, I've also become fond of the bottles, which seem to me a delightful throwback to a time of roosters crowing in the morn and the clink of a milkman arriving at the back door. Popping my nostalgic balloon is the prickly irritation of returning those empties along with managing the thick wad of dollar bills I accumulate as my bottle deposits (paid in plastic) come back to me as cash. For Lent a year ago, I took on this minor annoyance. I started folding the singles into packets of $3 each. I tuck one into my wallet and store the rest in the central storage bin of the car. Now, whenever I drive by a homeless soul on a street corner, rather than fumbling for the wallet in my back pocket (or often using that awkwardness as an excuse just to move on), I simply reach over as I roll down the window. I must remember that the homeless man on the street corner is dust, and to dust he shall return. The annoying mother and her three screaming children holding up the grocery store checkout line are dust, and to dust they shall return. And I too am dust, and to dust I shall return. You see, dust and ashes represent not just *memento mori*, not just reminders of our own mortality. Dust and ashes are the great equalizers. To this end we all come. In this, we are all the same. How, then, can we justify our condescension to others, our ill manners, our arrogant indifference? How can we who are dust and ashes be proud?

Lent 1

"One Art" by Elizabeth Bishop (1975)

The art of losing isn't hard to master;
so many things seem filled with the intent
to be lost that their loss is no disaster.   *line 3*

Lose something every day. Accept the fluster
of lost door keys, the hour badly spent.
The art of losing isn't hard to master.   *line 6*

Then practice losing farther, losing faster:
places, and names, and where it was you meant
to travel. None of these will bring disaster.   *line 9*

I lost my mother's watch. And look! my last, or
next-to-last, of three loved houses went.
The art of losing isn't hard to master.   *line 12*

I lost two cities, lovely ones. And, vaster,
some realms I owned, two rivers, a continent.
I miss them, but it wasn't a disaster.   *line 15*

—Even losing you (the joking voice, a gesture
I love) I shan't have lied. It's evident
the art of losing's not too hard to master
though it may look like (*Write* it!) like disaster.   *line 19*

You will find discussion questions for this poem on page 131.

This poem is a villanelle; if you haven't yet read about villanelle in the glossary, please go do so now. It will help very much in understanding some of what follows.

The Art of Losing: Following on the heels of "Ozymandias," we find in "One Art" another exploration of mutability. The persona in Bishop's poem focuses on personal loss, describing it as an art or a skill that can be improved with practice. Mastering this art begins by accepting the inevitable loss of just about everything ("so many things seem filled with the intent / to be lost"). The persona encourages his listeners to adopt an indifference to this inevitability. Loss is just no big deal, according to this speaker, "no disaster" (an attitude captured in another phrase I heard for the first time after I moved to the south: "ain't nothin' but a thing"). Part of the pleasure of the poem may be found in the persona's almost comical escalation of things that can be and have been lost, starting with small objects like car keys or a wasted hour or forgotten names (we've all been there), but rapidly scaling up to houses, cities, and entire continents that the persona has "lost" along the way. He misses things like his mother's watch and his former abodes, but he assures us that losing them "wasn't a disaster."

All things come of thee, O Lord: While we see very little in "One Art" that seems overtly spiritual (much less Christian), the attitude of the persona towards loss aligns with a Christian understanding that nothing we think is ours in this life really belongs to us: family heirlooms, cars, homes . . . nothing. You can't really lose what you haven't really owned. Note how the persona extends this attitude to include less material dimensions of our lives as well. "Where it was you meant / to travel," for instance, suggests that even our plans or hopes or dreams are not ours, not really. We have less control than we think, so why even kid ourselves about it? Let it go! Further, the persona's exhortation to pursue loss actively sounds much like a kind of Lenten discipline. Lose something every day! Since you are going to lose it all eventually, be proactive. It's good practice in mastering the art.

—Even losing you: The real power of the poem lies in the sudden reversal at line 16, accomplished through a variety of poetic devices. Notice for instance the dash at the beginning of the *quatrain*, indicating a pause there, as if the possibility of "losing you" brings the persona up short, makes him stop and consider. Note how the sudden intrusion of distracting parenthetical thoughts (the voice, a gesture) suddenly throws the persona off his smooth and overconfident delivery. See also how the repetition of line 1 has altered: "the art of losing isn't hard to master" has become "It's evident / the art of losing's not too hard to master." A couple of small yet artful changes signal the reader that this art may be more difficult to master than the persona has promised. The last line of the poem brings a final hesitation. The persona cannot bring himself to write the word "disaster" (a term he has used so glibly up to this point) in this new context of "losing you," and so he must admonish himself (*Write* it!), awkwardly repeating the word "like" before he can finally do it. It's evident that losing his beloved would indeed be something "like disaster." The sentiment explored here may be familiar (the loss of people, even if we acknowledge that they don't really "belong" to us, cannot be compared to the loss of things), but the *way* the poet portrays the persona's complex attitude gives enormous pleasure.

A biographical note that enriches our understanding of the poem: As I researched Elizabeth Bishop for this meditation, I found that her father died while she was still an infant and that her mother died in 1929 when Bishop was only eighteen. Clearly, Bishop experienced loss early in her life, and some readers, seeing the reference to "my mother's watch" in this poem, read it as semi-autobiographical, with the "you" in the final quatrain being a reference to the death of Bishop's mother. This may be so, but further investigation revealed to me an even more immediate context. Bishop penned "One Art" over the course of several weeks in 1975, during which she was estranged from her lover, Alice Methfessel. Lloyd Schwartz, a friend of Bishop (and my former poetry professor), has asserted that the poem is definitely about Methfessel, and "One Art" played a role in their ultimate reconciliation. (Please note that, despite this biographical context, we still should not treat the persona of "One Art" as if he were the poet. The speaker is still an artistic creation.) In this context, the repetition inherent in the *villanelle* comes across as desperation, the persona frantically attempting to convince us (and himself) that the art of losing really *is* easy to master and that losing even the person he loves more than anyone else in the world will not matter. Except he can't do it, and, in fact, the form of the villanelle won't *allow* him do it. The persona's destination (losing you would be a disaster to me) has been foreshadowed by the poem's villanelle structure all along. If you play by the rules, line 3 must be the final line. In "One Art," as in this world, disaster gets the last word.

It is true that "all things come from thee, and of thy own have we given thee" (1 Chronicles 29:14). And yes, it's equally true that, paraphrasing John, whoever loves his life too much in this world loses it, but whoever hates this life will keep his life in eternity (12:25). Nevertheless, I am grateful to Elizabeth Bishop for reminding us that even as we long for eternity, losing what we love is a talent rarely mastered. Despite ourselves, we fall in love with people and the places we share with them. We treasure mementoes we have inherited from parents and grandparents. We weep when we lose them. Ecclesiastes assures us that there will be a time for laughter, but also promises a time for tears. Inevitably, something we have taken for granted will fail. Ultimately, every heart will break. We cannot avoid the pain of loss, nor should we try to. There is no side-step to suffering (Anna Kamienska's artistic expression of this idea she called "A prayer that will be answered"). Though I may not fully understand why it should be so, this I have come firmly to believe: what I do with my pain (deny it, bury myself in it, embrace it, or transcend it) will become the single most important measure of my life. Welcome to the crash course in pain management we also sometimes call "Lent."

LENT 2

"Holy Sonnet 14" by John Donne (1610)

Batter my heart, three personed God; for you
As yet but knock, breathe, shine, and seek to mend;
That I may rise and stand, o'erthrow me, and bend
Your force, to break, blow, burn, and make me new.   *line 4*
   I, like an usurpt town, to another due,
   Labour to admit you, but oh, to no end,
   Reason, your viceroy in me, me should defend,
   But is captived, and proves weak or untrue.   *line 8*
Yet dearly I love you, and would be loved fain*,
But am betrothed unto your enemy:
Divorce me, untie, or break that knot again;
Take me to you, imprison me, for I   *line 12*
   Except you enthrall me, never shall be free,
   Nor ever chaste, except you ravish me.

fain: happily or eagerly

You will find discussion questions for this poem on page 132.

Introduction: In Mark, chapter 9, the father of an epileptic child about to be healed by Jesus cries out, "I believe; help my unbelief!" (24). Many, many poems in this volume explore this struggle of faith. We believe, yet given our fallen human natures and our self-centered tendencies, we cannot maintain faith on our own. In his "Holy Sonnet 14," John Donne acknowledges this shortcoming and takes the solution to the next level. Not content with periodic reminders of God's love (as in the case of, say, Shakespeare's "Sonnet 29"), this persona implores God to possess her heart completely. Only then, she paradoxically claims, might she attain total freedom from the slavery of her own nature.

Violent Imagery: We are reading a *sonnet*, and, following the sonnet structure, the poem can be neatly divided into three parts:

1. The first *quatrain*: "I am a flawed vessel that must be destroyed and remade."
2. The second *quatrain*: "I am an occupied town that you, God, must liberate."
3. The *sestet*: "I am betrothed to sinfulness; you must break that bond and possess me completely in order to keep me from returning to that bad relationship."

Focusing for now on the first quatrain, some readers might be taken aback by the violence of the imagery. The persona asks God to "batter" her heart. She imagines herself as a flawed glass or metal vessel that must be melted down and remade. She implores God to "break" her apart; "blow" air across the fire to intensify the heat; "burn" away her impurities; "and make [her] new."[1] The alliteration of these verbs ("batter," "bend," "break," "blow," and "burn") emphasizes the explosive, destructive nature of the action. While this violence may be off-putting for some, it does participate in a New Testament theology which suggests that to live in Christ we must die with him. Paul writes that "we know that our old self was crucified with him so that the sinful body might be destroyed, and we might no longer be enslaved to sin" (Romans 6:6). Understanding this poem requires us to absorb one of the ideas Paul expresses here: we are *slaves* to our own sinfulness. Imagine us as glass vessels, then sin represents a flaw in the very material of our being. Imagine us each as a town, then sin has settled in for the duration. What's more, we secretly (or maybe not so secretly) find our own sinfulness *attractive*. It's the bad boy we know we should shun, and yet we return to him time and time again. Sometimes only

---

1. I am reminded of Isaiah 64:8 ("O Lord, thou art our Father; we are the clay, and thou art our potter; we are all the work of thy hand.") See also Paul's description of our bodies as "earthen vessels" (2 Corinthians 4:7).

an abruptly dramatic intervention can break a cycle of addiction, and as we look again at the verbs Paul has used ("enslaved," "crucify," "destroy"), perhaps Donne's powerful imagery doesn't seem so very inappropriate. After all, Christ's intervention for us involved thorns, lashes, nails, and the point of a spear.

Jerusalem, Jerusalem: The fairly straightforward second *quatrain* leads us directly to the book of Lamentations (yes, that's exactly what you were thinking, right?). In these four lines, the persona imagines herself as a city that wants to admit God, but an enemy force occupies her completely. If we can imagine any biblical city in a fallen relationship with God, that city must be Jerusalem. In Lamentations, we see Jerusalem portrayed as a woman who has been unfaithful: "Jerusalem sinned grievously, therefore she became filthy; . . . she took no thought of her doom; therefore her fall is terrible. . . . O Lord, behold my affliction, for the enemy has triumphed!" (Lamentations 1:8–9). Of course, we cannot forget that Jerusalem welcomed Jesus on Palm Sunday, only to crucify him days later: "Jerusalem, Jerusalem," Jesus cries, "killing the prophets and stoning those who are sent to you!" (Luke 13:34). So what might appear to be a rather random simile (sinful person equals occupied town) actually participates in Biblical imagery of a city that yearns for God and yet rejects and betrays him as well. In "Holy Sonnet 14," Donne places this image perfectly to segue into the final six lines, for the Bible indicates that the relationship between God and City will only be restored at the second coming: "And I saw the holy city, new Jerusalem, coming down out of heaven from God, prepared as a bride adorned for her husband" (Revelation 21:2). In this context, how startling might we find lines 9 and 10 of the "Holy Sonnet 14": we find the town, which should be adorned as a bride for her intended, actually betrothed to some interloper! And further, she seems powerless to break that engagement herself! Not exactly what the bridegroom was expecting, I should think.[2]

---

2. We might also note that God's relationship with Jerusalem can be restored only if the city is made new; thus, we might see a subtle connection between the second quatrain and the first. The persona's pleas to God to "o'erthrow me, and bend / Your force to break, blow, burn, and make me new," if imagined as the voice of the city, creates a context in which "batter" takes on the additional connotation of "battering ram."

For all of the poem's fine metaphorical developments in its first eight lines, at the heart of the poem lies the intimate relationship between the persona and God. As Christians, we understand that in baptism we metaphorically die with Christ in order to rise with him into a totally new life. It is not inappropriate to imagine this relationship in the most intimate of terms. Turning one last time to Paul, he writes in Romans that we have become dead to the law (of men) through the body of Christ, so "that [we] should be married to another, even to him who is raised from the dead, that we should bring forth fruit unto God" (7:4, KJV). Throughout the poem, the persona acknowledges that her flaws stand in the way of this perfect union. Ironically, she realizes that only *his* power can divorce her from it, can sever the knot which binds her to her sinful nature, so that she might then enter into this intimate communion with him. "Take me to you," she implores, and in the context of the violent imagery of this sonnet we must understand that for Donne's audience, "ravish" was also synonymous with "rape." For modern readers, this final line might take us right up to the edge of good taste (for some, maybe over the edge), but consider how carefully we have been prepared for this conclusion. From the very beginning, the persona has acknowledged a desperate desire for the love of God within the context of her own utter inability to sustain the relationship by herself. She knows that the power of God—and only the power of God—can provide the will to sustain this holy bond. Thus, by the end, she maintains the paradox that runs through the entire poem: destroy me, so that I may be made new; enthrall me, that I may be free from sin; and ravish me, that I may be spiritually pure.

Going too far? "Holy Sonnet 14" is a prayer to God. But will it be answered? I wonder if the extremity of the final lines may well be intentional. I do not believe it is in God's nature to ravish, in any sense of the term. We must choose fidelity. In fact, choice represents fidelity's greatest challenge and its greatest joy. In all relationships, we must find the strength to act in ways consistent with and faithful to the promises we have made. Our human failings of jealousy, anger, impatience, and ingratitude will present obstacles to our vows, but not insurmountable ones. To experience—nay, to embrace—these shortcomings and learn how to live with and control them ultimately strengthens our bonds of faith. I have to wonder, therefore, if the persona's exhortations at the end (imprison me; hold me in thrall, ravish me), while understandable, even familiar, represent bootless cries to deaf heaven. Donne emphasizes the persona's passivity through what I consider an "inert" *chiasmus* in the poem's final two lines:

> A. Except you enthrall me,
>   B. **Never** shall be **free**,
>   B. Nor **ever chaste**,
> A. Except you ravish me.

This chiasmus suggests repetition only, with no development or transformation, and the repeated negatives seem strangely paralyzing. The persona has completely objectified herself (the objective case "me" repeats five times in the last four lines, while the subjective case "I" occurs once, buried at the end of line 12), and she places the agency to act on God and God alone. But God doesn't want passive automatons, he wants and loves living, breathing, struggling human beings, warts and all. He wants us to fall in love with him of our own free will and to stay with him because we love him, not because we have been taken prisoner by him. It may be impossible for us to remain true by ourselves ("help my unbelief"), but we cannot ask God to bear the burden of us unless we will freely choose to bear the burden of God as well (we will see this dynamic again in our Palm Sunday poem, "The Donkey").

Returning to the first two lines of "Holy Sonnet 14," I'll take the odds that God will hold the course with his current strategy. He does not batter hearts, but he does knock on them. He does not break down doors, but he will stand on the threshold (another *threshold*!), waiting for an invitation. He will not possess our souls, but when we falter, "weak or untrue," he will be ever present, ready to forgive the contrite heart. Ultimately, and ironically, the second line of Donne's sonnet may be its most important. Christ does not change. He seeks always to mend our broken relationships with him, but we must decide, invite, remain, and embrace our share of the hard work as well. As I have said before, faith brings not serenity. And that's about as Lenten a message as you are likely to hear.

LENT 3
"A prayer that will be answered"
by Anna Kamieńska

Lord let me suffer much
and then let me die

Let me walk through the quiet
May nothing remain behind me not even fear   *line 4*

Grant that the world continue as before
let the sea kiss the shore

Let the grass continue to be green
so that a frog can hide in it   *line 8*
so that someone can bury her face in it
and weep until emptied of love

Grant that a day will rise so bright
as if there were no more suffering   *line 12*

And may my poem stand transparent as a windowpane
Against which a stray bee bumps his head

Translated from the original Polish by Monica Pawinski and Dave Worster

You will find discussion questions for this poem on page 134.

Anna Kamieńska lived and died in Poland, 1920–1986. She survived the misery of World War II, obviously, and the terror of the Soviet occupation. Her husband Jan died suddenly of cancer in 1967, after which her Christian faith deepened (although, as a very intelligent and rational person, she constantly struggled with the irrationality of faith). She wrote over a dozen books of poetry, and at least two volumes of her Notebooks have been published, as well as other writings. Why she is not better known in this country is a mystery to me.

I first encountered "A prayer that will be answered" in a collection called *Astonishments: Selected Poems of Anna Kamienska*, edited and translated by Grazyna Drabik and David Curzon. While I was blown away by the ideas and intersessions expressed in the poem, some of the individual lines (with all respect to the translators) were to me unbearably clunky. So I went where we go in the twenty-first century, the Internet. There I discovered one or two more translations, but again, nothing that really sang to me as poetry in English. Finally, I stumbled upon the work in its original Polish, and I had a thought: why not find someone fluent in the language and take a shot at our own translation? I connected with the wonderful Monica Pawinski through a mutual friend, and the result you see above. The work of translation was far more difficult than I anticipated (so I look at others' work in a far more sympathetic light now), but Monica, ever cheerful and open minded, still made the task a joy. Because of the wonderful way "A prayer that will be answered" unfolds, I intend to depart from the format you have seen in earlier meditations, instead progressing through the poem couplet by couplet (more or less). Because of the unique context, I will also offer comments about translating from the original Polish when it seems helpful or relevant to do so.

1. Lord let me suffer much / and then let me die: No other work in this collection except Shakespeare's "Sonnet 15" reminds me more strongly of the Teacher of Ecclesiastes than this poem. In "A prayer that will be answered," the persona assures us that we will each experience a time to weep, a time to mourn, and a time to die. Frail and fragile creatures, we will none of us escape this world without sickness or injury or grief. The first two lines of the poem also remind me of a Chekhov play called *The Seagull*. In response to the question of why she always wears black, a character named Masha replies: "I'm in mourning for my life." Masha seems an ambulatory embodiment of the sentiment "to be born is to begin to die." Pretty bleak philosophy, isn't it? Or is it? If physical or emotional pain and suffering are truly unavoidable facets of life, why do we think it odd or morbid to think on them?

The ancient Greek philosopher Epictetus once wrote: "Let death be daily before your eyes, and you will never entertain any abject thought, nor too eagerly covet anything." We really want to consider this statement as sort of counter-intuitive, don't we? How can remembering death every day banish abject thoughts? After reading his words, you will be unastonished to learn that Epictetus taught and practiced a stoic way of life. Stoics, for those who don't know, believed that external events lie, generally speaking, beyond our control and that our suffering occurs from trying to assert our wills at times when we have no power to do so (or, conversely, by neglecting what we *can* control, namely our own responses to these external events). Stoicism teaches us to accept whatever happens calmly and to respond to it appropriately. Let go of whatever you cannot rule, but act where you can. The British have an expression for this: "Keep calm and carry on."

At any rate, what a great line from Epictetus: "Let death be daily before your eyes!" Remember that this life does not last. Literary critics have a term for this reminder, *memento mori* (remember your ending day). We encountered this idea already while reading "Ozymandias": remember you are dust, and to dust you shall return. If not carried to a grief-ridden extreme ("I'm in mourning for my life"), this attitude might actually help us live better today. Epictetus believed that this reminder would keep us not only from greed (Why accumulate material possessions that you will eventually lose? This question reminds me of "One Art.") but also from depression. He believed that *memento mori* could serve to heighten one's appreciation of the present moment, a wake-up call to live each day with joy in the face of mortality.

2. Let me walk through the quiet / May nothing remain behind me not even fear: The final Polish word in line 3, "cisze," may be translated as "silence" or "quiet." Monica and I chose "quiet" for the "k" and "w" sounds it shares with "walk." What does the persona mean by "the quiet," and what does a walk through the quiet actually mean? Many of us spend much of our existence in solitude and silence. No less a figure than Theodor Geisel (Dr. Seuss) reminds us that, "[w]hether we like it or not, / Alone is something you'll be quite a lot." So "the quiet" could be a metaphor for life; yet, given that line 3 immediately follows line 2, with its clear reference to death, and given the reference in line 4 to leaving nothing behind, which suggests departure, I believe this walk through the quiet represents that final, *liminal* crossing of the threshold, the walk through the valley of the shadow of death. Our loved ones cannot take these steps with us, nor would we want them to, but we hope to meet another friend along the way.

The persona embraces the quiet without complaint or protest, asking only that the Lord permit him to walk through it with all his own baggage, leaving none of his burdens for others to bear (the Polish phrase in line 4 "zostanie po mnie" can also imply a legacy, something one does leave behind when one dies). Note the one and only burden that merits specific mention: fear. Like suffering and death, "let me be afraid" is a prayer that will be answered for us all. We will experience fear of the unknown, fear of failure, fear of loss, fear of pain and suffering, and fear of death, not to mention myriad idiosyncratic phobias. I love line 4 for the serenity with which the persona asks that he may take complete ownership of his own inexorable anxieties and also his wish to take all that trepidation with him when he goes. He asks God for the grace to die so well that for those who witness this death, no fear of death remains to haunt them, just a legacy of forbearance and peace.

3. Grant that the world continue as before / let the sea kiss the shore / Let the grass continue to be green (I've clustered these next three lines together instead of a couplet because I think these three lines set us up for the next three lines): The Polish verb at the beginning of line 5, "spraw," is not a commonly used word. "The only place I remember hearing it is at Mass," writes Monica, "when the prayer is a petition to God the Father, an asking for permission from an authority figure." While "make" is also a fitting translation, we decided to go for the less common term, "grant," both as more fitting perhaps for a petition and also for the assonance of the phrase "grant that." Thus the line amounts to more than just passive acceptance that "life goes on," it is a fervent prayer that life should do so. The same verb appears in line 10, and we have chosen "grant" there again, but have used it nowhere else in the poem.

I love the image of the sea kissing the shore. Not only does it create in the reader's mind a recollection of waves gently rolling into the sand

and the comforting lull of the surf, it also conjures reminiscences of the passage of time. Let the tides go out, the persona might be asking, and then let them come back in again. It also delights me that the persona calls for the grass to remain green as he departs. No longing for brown dryness here, no indulging in autumnal imagery of yellowed leaves, no iron gray skies, no sorrowful falling rain. As the persona prays below, let the sun continue its daily round, or as the Teacher of Ecclesiastes might say, let each season keep its appointed place in the cycle. If it is time for the grass to be green, then please just let it be green.

4. so that a frog can hide in it / so that someone can bury her face in it / and weep until emptied of love: Just when we might think we have this persona figured out, he takes an unexpected turn. We think we've got him nailed: a stoic who asks God only that he may depart this world with quiet dignity while the great globe goes spinning on after his death. Then we experience a shift precisely halfway through the poem: *Let the grass continue to be green . . . so that a frog can hide in it*. In addition to a prayer for the maintenance of seasonal progression, the persona also asks that the grass remain green so that it will continue to serve as good camouflage for green frogs. Why must frogs hide in this green grass? To avoid predators, we must presume. Frogs don't like to be eaten. Frogs hide because of instinctual fear. Despite the persona's prayer that he leave nothing behind, not even fear, he knows that fear will always remain behind. God may grant him his request to carry his own anxieties with him as he goes, but he cannot redeem those who remain behind from suffering or heartbreak. He really can't take any of that with him. So he asks also that the grass stay green so that some future heartbroken lover may one day bury her face in it and weep until utterly emptied.

5. Grant that a day will rise so bright / as if there were no more suffering: Pain and suffering will not end with the departure of the persona, but we do not have to submit to it. The sun will rise tomorrow, bringing with it hope for a new day. The persona is not the world's savior, but we do have one, and in the religious context of the poem, it's not difficult to see the brightly rising day as a *sunrise / son rise* metaphor. In fact, we could interpret lines 9 through 11, with the progression of ideas that move from burial to emptiness to rising, as presenting an image of death, a vacant tomb, and resurrection. With the Teacher of

Ecclesiastes, Kamienska's persona acknowledges the labor and sorrow in our lives, but also expresses the idea and the hope for eternity God has given each of us. I once asked a jovial friend of mine how he maintained his (sometimes relentlessly) positive attitude, and he replied: "I get up every day remembering that my redeemer lives." As we near the conclusion of this fantastic poem, we begin to perceive its remarkable one-two punch: "I know that I will suffer and die; I also know that my redeemer lives."

It seems almost inevitable that, when one speaks of suffering in a biblical context, one must turn to Job. So I'll defy convention. I think an equally illustrative example of how to understand suffering comes from another source: Genesis and the story of Joseph. Sold into slavery by his own brothers, falsely accused and imprisoned in Egypt, Joseph endures this injustice and ultimately perseveres, serving as governor to Pharaoh. As such, he eventually finds himself in a position to revenge himself upon his brothers and their families. Joseph chooses instead to see a larger, more merciful picture: "You intended to harm me," he says to his brothers, "but God intended it for good to accomplish what is now being done, the saving of many lives. So therefore, do not be afraid. I will provide for you and your little ones" (Genesis 50:19–21, NIV). Joseph could see that, while the world is filled with hatred, jealousy, betrayal, and injustice, much of it "undeserved" according to our puny sense of right and wrong, God works to bend all those human frailties to her good purposes.

More important, God has taken all this suffering upon herself in the person of Jesus Christ. Job, in his agony, could only long for a mediator: "If only there were someone to mediate between us, someone to bring us together, someone to remove God's rod from me, so that his terror would frighten me no more" (Job 9:33, NIV, and so much for defying convention). We are much more fortunate. In fact, really, the only way we can understand evil and pain in a fallen world is to abide in the transformative miracle of the cross and the tomb. We might understand the passion as an act of re-creation: Christ took emotional agony, physical torment, and death, and he made them a door into eternity. We see this transformation suggested in lines 9 through 12 of "A prayer that will be answered." The persona prays that the grief and desolation described in lines 9 and 10 will be redeemed by the sunrise and healing balm he imagines in lines 11 and 12. The suffering he embraces in line 1 ("cierpiec") is no more by line 12 ("nie bylo cierpienia").

6. And may my poem stand transparent as a windowpane / Against which a stray bee bumps his head: I love these final two lines. Let's face it, we've been managing some pretty heavy lifting in this poem: fear and heartbreak, suffering and death. In line 13, it seems as though the persona and the poet merge, and, just as Christ's sacrifice has transformed suffering and death into hope and new life, the persona/poet asks that her poem might do the same, that she might, through her own act of imagination and creativity, bring clarity to others. It has certainly helped bring clarity to me. There can be no firmer daily reminder of death than a sentence of metastasized cancer. Despite advances in research and hope for a medical miracle, the regular appointments, lab tests, injections, and pills keep always before me the knell of Ash Wednesday. I have been gravely tempted to abandon myself to my grief. My sense of loss at times crashes over me with the overwhelming, irresistible force of the sea. I have wanted, in other words, to go into mourning for my life. This poem has sharply reminded me of why this is such folly. Hamlet says to Horatio late in his eponymous play: "Since no man of aught he leaves knows, what is it to leave betimes?" Paraphrased: "Since no man knows when he is destined to die, what does it mean to die early?" This poem has reminded me that God promises none of us a life of any particular length or quality. It has reminded me that cancer itself is not of central importance; my response is what matters. Pain Management. A year before he died of cancer at age 49, Stuart Scott said, "When you die, it does not mean you lose to cancer. You beat cancer by how you live, why you live, and in the manner in which you live. So live." Like Stuart and Joseph, I must ask how I can, with God's help, work to bend this adversity to his good purposes, how I might render pain into clarity. This poem has been for me, indeed, a windowpane through which I see the day brightly rising.[1]

---

1. A different path to the same understanding: Stanislaw Baranczak and Clare Cavanagh translate lines 12 and 13 like this: "as if there were no more *pain* / And let my poem stand clear as a windowpane" (emphasis added). While "pain" could be seen as a loose translation of "cierpiec," I love how that choice literally reveals the transformation of suffering ("pain") into clarity ("pane").

In that context, I can very much appreciate the whimsical humor we also see in these final two lines. The light touch of the final line especially comes as an unexpected, yet welcome, relief. Just as we are imagining a transparent windowpane as a glorious positive, it becomes an invisible hazard for the unsuspecting bee. In this world, even clarity can be dangerous! Not to push it too far, but I think even this final image participates in the overall stoicism of the poem. Imagine this bee, flying along and minding its own business, suddenly encountering a literally unforeseen crisis. He might bump up against the window a couple of times . . . to no avail. Then, perhaps realizing he has no control over this situation, he just chooses another way around and soldiers on, with maybe just a bit of a headache. After all, he has nectar to gather, the next flower to pollinate, and honey to make. I can relate. Keep calm and carry on.

PALM SUNDAY

"The Donkey" by G. K. Chesterton (1900)

When fishes flew and forests walked
And figs grew upon thorn,
Some moment when the moon was blood
Then surely I was born.   *line 4*
With monstrous head and sickening cry
And ears like errant wings,
The devil's walking parody
On all four-footed things.   *line 8*
The tattered outlaw of the earth,
Of ancient crooked will;
Starve, scourge, deride me: I am dumb,
I keep my secret still.   *line 12*
Fools! For I also had my hour;
One far fierce hour and sweet:
There was a shout about my ears,
And palms before my feet.   *line 16*

You will find discussion questions for this poem on page 135.

Rejoice greatly, O daughter of Zion! Shout aloud, O daughter of Jerusalem! Lo, your king comes to you; triumphant and victorious is he, humble, and riding on an ass. (Zechariah 9:9)

The destiny of a donkey: On the day he was to enter Jerusalem for the final time, Jesus sent two disciples into a village. There, he assured them, they would find an ass "on which no one has ever yet sat" (Luke 19 and Mark 11). He instructed them to bring the ass to him, and he rode it triumphantly into the city, surrounded by some of the very same people who would turn against him in a matter of days. How intrigued I've become by the story of this animal. Zechariah foretells her appearance, and Jesus sends disciples to find her, knowing she would be waiting for her first rider, ready to fulfill her destiny. We know not where she comes from or what happens to her after. She appears as needed to play her foretold role in the story, and then she vanishes. "The Donkey," remarkable for its early images suggesting ancient magic and primeval mystery, offers a unique (for this collection) persona: a talking animal. The birth of the donkey is portentous; her voice, bitter and self-deprecating; and her listeners, scorned as ignorant fools. In form, the poem seems simple, four quatrains with an alternating rhyme, yet the opaque depths of "The Donkey" defy clear and linear explication.

Birth: While the first stanza as a whole, describing the moment of the donkey's birth, contains a couple of clear biblical *allusions*, the first line remains obscure. What does it mean? When did fish fly? When did forests ever walk? Walking trees remind me of two cultural references steeped in legend and prophecy: the Ents in J.R.R. Tolkien's *The Lord of the Rings* and mobile Birnam Wood in Shakespeare's *Macbeth*. In the former, the legendary Ents not only really exist (much to the astonishment of several characters in the book), but also will play a key role in the (spoiler alert) victory of good over evil. In the latter, a prophetic apparition assures Macbeth that he "shall never vanquished be, until / Great Birnam wood to high Dunsinane hill [his seat of power] / Shall come against him." Macbeth seizes upon this (ultimately deceptive) reassurance of security: "That will never be: / Who can impress the forest; bid the tree / Unfix his earth-bound root?" (4.1.92–96). Macbeth thinks a walking forest impossible, fantastical, until it happens, until this unlikely prophecy actually comes true. The fulfillment of prophecy is part and parcel of "The Donkey," and line 1 of the poem invites us into a world of supernatural possibilities. The donkey is born into this time before fish were limited to water and forests rooted to a single spot. Before animals went mute. Indeed, certain magical, mystical elements in "The Donkey" remind me powerfully of the legends we find in "The Oxen," and I am struck by the connection between hallowed Christmas Eve (marking Christ's entrance into creation) and Holy Palm Sunday (marking Christ's entrance into Jerusalem).

The imagery of the poem does not move us only backward through time. Line 3 offers an omen or portent (a blood red moon typically taken to foretell danger, death, or bloodshed) that directs our gaze into the future. The Book of Revelation, after the Lamb opens the sixth seal, commands us to "behold, there was a great earthquake; and the sun became black as sackcloth, the full moon became like blood, and the stars of the sky fell to the earth as the fig tree sheds its winter fruit when shaken by a gale" (6:12–13). The blood-red moon signals the Second Coming, and in the same chapter of Revelation people of all social classes seek to hide from the judgment of God, for their lack of faith will exclude them from salvation. Thus, lines 3 and 4 may be seen as moving in two temporal directions: backward to the day of the donkey's birth, but also forward to the day of Christ's return.

In the context of line 2 of "The Donkey," I find it an interesting coincidence that the Revelation verses also mention the fruit of the fig tree. Figs growing upon thorns must deliberately reference a teaching of Jesus we find in both Matthew and Luke. In Matthew, Jesus says: "Beware of false prophets, who come to you in sheep's clothing but inwardly are ravenous wolves. You will know them by their fruits. Are grapes gathered from thorns, or figs from thistles? So, every sound tree bears good fruit, but the bad tree bears evil fruit" (7:15–17). Luke's version of this moment renders the poem's *allusion* even more clear: "for each tree is known by its own fruit. For *figs are not gathered from thorns*, nor are grapes picked from a bramble bush" (6:44, emphasis added). Jesus makes this comment in the course of what some call the Sermon on the Plain. Earlier in chapter 6, he offers multiple lessons on humility, including one so clearly relevant to this poem: "Blessed are you that weep now, for you shall laugh. Blessed are you when men hate you, and when they exclude you and revile you, and cast out your name as evil, on account of the Son of man! Rejoice in that day, and leap for joy, for behold, your reward is great in heaven; for so their fathers did to the prophets" (Luke 6:21–23). Just as others scorned and reviled the prophets of old, the donkey (a prophet in her own right) feels also outcast and derided, yet she knows that her Ecclesiastical season of sorrow will someday yield a season of joy.

The tattered outlaw of the earth: I find myself both taken aback and intrigued by the extreme self-deprecation of lines 5 through 12.

The donkey calls her head "monstrous," her voice "sickening," and her ears "like errant wings." (This phrase makes me think of fallen angels, for who else had wings that went astray?) This odd thought seems validated by the next line, in which the donkey describes herself as the devil's walking parody, a creature of Lucifer himself, a poor imitation of God's creation. She continues through the third stanza: as a "tattered outlaw" (like Cain?), she feels she deserves mockery, scorn, and exile. Other than the (somewhat inexplicable) self-loathing, what else is going on here? The persona tells her audience, starve me, scourge me, deride me, I will bear it all in silence, and I will keep my secrets. As her painful defiance rises from the page, though, it seems to me that another presence, a presence that has hovered in the background of the poem right from the beginning, emerges to take the donkey's burdens as his own. For who else becomes a tattered outlaw through the course of Holy Week? Who else is scourged and ridiculed? Who remains silent before the High Priest and his false accusations?

This humble creature, this willing servant, celebrates with Christ his moment of triumph. With hosannas ringing in their ears and palm branches and garments spread before them, together they enter Jerusalem. But she also endures with him debasement and abuse, the scorn of the crowd, and physical suffering that she does not deserve. This is the subject of Chesterton's poem: the tribulation and the joy of bearing the burden of Christ. Carrying him can be difficult, to say the least, and often downright terrifying, so fearful that even those who knew and loved him best sometimes found it more than they could bear. The days of Holy Week abound in examples of betrayal and denial, yet Jesus once preached: "Come to me, all who labor and are heavy laden, and I will give you rest. Take my yoke upon you, and learn from me; for I am gentle and lowly in heart, and you will find rest for your souls. For my yoke is easy, and my burden is light" (Matthew 11:28–30). Huh? Given our witness of Holy Week, how can we possibly imagine this burden of Christianity as easy or light? Note Christ's emphasis on humility: learn from me gentleness and lowliness of heart. We cannot come to Jesus filled with self-confidence, knowing that our strength or our intelligence will suffice to bear this burden or keep this faith on our own. No, we must come like the lowly donkey, acknowledging our monstrosities and deformities and asking, even as we take on the yoke of Christ, for him to take on the yoke of us. The burden of Christ is not light because *we* are strong; it's light because *he* is.

The persona of "A prayer that will be answered" looks to hope beyond her suffering, and the donkey does the same. She describes the events of Palm Sunday as a distant, treasured memory: "One far fierce hour and sweet." Yet, as we have seen, the poem is unrestrained by time or space. This donkey is a prophet. The *allusions* to Holy Week and Revelation suggest that there will come a day, some moment when the moon looks red like blood, when the earth will tremble, and the stars will fall from the sky. When that time comes, perhaps, this outcast donkey will bear her burden once again, rejoicing as she carries her savior through the gates and onto the streets of a New Jerusalem. *Hosannah in the highest.*

MAUNDY THURSDAY

"Those Winter Sundays"
by Robert Hayden (1962)

Sundays too my father got up early
and put his clothes on in the blueblack cold,
then with cracked hands that ached
with labor in the weekday weather made
banked fires blaze. No one ever thanked him.   *line 5*

I'd wake and hear the cold splintering, breaking.
When the rooms were warm, he'd call,
and slowly I would rise and dress,
fearing the chronic angers of that house.   *line 9*

Speaking indifferently to him,
who had driven out the cold
and polished my good shoes as well.
What did I know, what did I know
of love's austere and lonely offices?   *line 14*

You will find discussion questions for this poem on page 136.

For reasons I cannot rationally explain, it is impossible for me to imagine this speaker as a daughter; therefore, I am presenting the persona as a male throughout below.

"Those Winter Sundays" offers a memory of love and devotion. Not the kind of devotion some poets write of, the "I'll love you 'til the stars fall from the sky" variety, but rather the very real, nitty-gritty, food-on-the-table and roof-over-your-head kind of commitment. This love does not declare itself from the mountaintop or beat its breast on a street corner, but rather manifests in a thousand decidedly unglamorous and unspectacular ways, from packing your daily lunchbox to washing your clothes to rising early to start a fire so the floor feels warm to your feet.

The blueblack cold: Through the first seven lines of the poem, the persona beautifully lays out the nature of his father's devotion in details that vividly recall those frigid winter mornings. The most important word in line 1 of the poem, "too," strongly suggests that the father also got up early *every* morning of the week, never earning a break from his responsibilities, not even on the traditional "day of rest." I love how the persona recalls the father's hands as cracked and aching from his "labor in the weekday weather," indicating that he works outside for a living. The persona's vivid recollection of the cold foregrounds the onerous nature of the father's morning routine. In line 2, for instance, cold has color (a bruising "blueblack"), and in line 6 it has material existence. The persona imagines he can hear the cold splintering and breaking as if it were ice thawing as the warmth of the fire spreads throughout the house. The sounds we hear support the imagery: the *consonance* of repeated "k"s and "d"s (bluebla**ck**, **cracked**, a**ched**, wee**kd**ay, ban**ked**, than**ked**, brea**k**ing) creates lines that literally crackle. These sounds echo the cracking joints of the father's aching hands as he goes about his tasks, or the crackling, popping fire he kindles, or the splintering, breaking cold, or perhaps all three in succession.

No one ever thanked him: Through the middle of the poem, the focus shifts from the father's work to the persona's attitude about his memories. I believe that ultimately the son feels grief and regret for the way he might have treated his father, though if this be so, he sidles his way into these emotions and never clearly articulates them. Emotional distance is a hallmark of the poem. Take, for instance, the end of line 5: "No one ever thanked him." As we consider this line, we have to ask, how can the persona *know* that no one else in the house ever thanked the father? He can't. So what does he really mean by this line? He means: "I never thanked him," but he cannot (or will not) say that. As was the case in "A prayer that will be answered," the first emotion literally evoked in "Those Winter Sundays" is fear, but note again how oddly the persona phrases the feeling: "fearing the chronic angers of that house." He attributes this anger, not to any specific individual, but rather to the whole building. Since a house cannot literally feel anything, and given the plural form of "angers," we could understand the line as something like "the chronic angers of various people who lived inside that house," but the persona cannot bring himself to even that level of specific emotional detail, much less reveal who was angry and why. Finally, of course we cannot assume that the father bears no responsibility for this tense situation. A day laborer who never gets a break from working may very well harbor his own simmering angers and resentments.

Emotional Distance: The persona describes himself as speaking indifferently to his father (an emotional chill never entirely driven out of the poem), and we recognize the distance also suggested by the father's wake-up call (he does not enter the bedroom or gently touch the child; rather, he calls from another part of the house). Until the final three lines, the persona holds this memory at arm's length (even the title reinforces distance: *those* winter Sundays feel farther away than, say, *these* winter Sundays). Interestingly, a seemingly random detail near the end pushes the persona past a certain emotional threshold. He holds himself together through the description of the father's task stirring to life the morning's fire, but his recollection that his father also took the time to polish his good shoes with those weather-beaten hands seems to crack the frozen armor of his indifference, releasing a suppressed wellspring of acknowledgement and regret. The persona's cry of remorse may be heard in the *assonance* of the final two lines, the repeated long "o"s creating a literal moan:

> *What did I know, what did I know / of love's austere and lonely offices?*

Now, granted, the persona does not suffer a complete emotional melt-down. We see no explicit apology ("Sorry that I never thanked you, Dad"); nor do we read anything like a *mea culpa* ("I share the blame for the anger and indifference in the house"). We do, however, witness a powerful recognition that his father loved him and got up early to start the fire *because* he loved him. I find it fascinating that the emotionally triggering detail is, of all possibilities, the polishing of shoes, and I cannot help but read this act on the part of the father as a metaphorical foot-washing. This parent, motivated by love, in the cold and lonely silence of a winter's morning, performed the weekly office of polishing his son's shoes. His son never thanked him for that task, but he did it nonetheless, Sunday after Sunday.

His father's voice: Forgive the lengthy passage, but this poem reminds me so strongly of Christ's example of servant ministry the night before his death that it warrants a full hearing: "Jesus, knowing that the Father had given all things into his hands, and that he had come from God and was going to God, rose from supper, laid aside his garments, and girded himself with a towel. Then he poured water into a basin and began to wash the disciples' feet, and to wipe them with the towel with which he was girded. He came to Simon Peter; and Peter said to him, 'Lord, do you wash my feet?' Jesus answered him, 'What I am doing you do not know now, but afterward you will understand.' . . . When he had washed their feet, and taken his garments, and resumed his place, he said to them, 'Do you know what I have done to you? You call me Teacher and Lord, and you are right, for so I am. If I then, your Lord and Teacher, have washed your feet, you also ought to wash one another's feet. For I have given you an example, that you also should do as I have done to you'" (John 13:3–15).

In the middle of "Those Winter Sundays" (a sonnet, we should note, a traditional format for the expression of love), the persona remembers hearing his father's call from a distance. In point of fact, the son hears that voice still, reverberating through all the intervening years. This haunting sonnet, with its slightly irregular structure, represents a perfectly imperfect form within which to portray this uncomfortable, yet oddly cherished, memory. He hears his father's call; he rises and remembers his father's austere service. *Father, do you wash my feet?* As the persona belatedly acknowledges his ingratitude and recognizes his father's steadfast love and devotion, he fulfills the prophecy of Jesus: *afterward, you will understand.* The beautiful, evocative poem by Robert Hayden becomes a gently powerful thanksgiving paean to all dedicated caregivers, all lonely performers of thankless daily tasks and offices, and all those who would follow in the footsteps of the servant-leader Jesus. *Yes, my son, I have given you an example, that you should also do what I have done.*

GOOD FRIDAY

"The Scattered Congregation"
by Tomas Transtromer (1973)

1.
We got ready and showed our home.
The visitor thought: you live well.
The slum must be inside you.   *line 3*

2.
Inside the church, pillars and vaulting
white as plaster, like the cast
around the broken arm of faith.   *line 6*

3.
Inside the church there's a begging bowl
that slowly lifts from the floor
and floats along the pews.   *line 9*

4.
But the church bells have gone underground.
They're hanging in the sewage pipes.
Whenever we take a step, they ring.   *line 12*

5.
Nicodemus the sleepwalker is on his way
to the Address. Who's got the Address?
Don't know. But that's where we're going.   *line 15*

You will find discussion questions for this poem on page 137.

Questions: In "The Scattered Congregation," we confront a challenging work, one of the most demanding in this book. As we complete our first reading, I think a number of questions will rise irresistibly in our minds: Who is showing their home, and why? Why does the visitor think these home-sellers must have a "slum" inside of them? What kind of attitude is suggested by a phrase like "the broken arm of faith"? Why does the persona imagine a begging bowl floating along the pews? Why have the church bells "gone underground"? These images pull and push us in multiple directions (perhaps an intentional movement working off the scattering mentioned in the poem's title?), and words like "broken" and "underground" create a general sense of unease.

Stanza 5 is the key: We encounter at last some context that might help us out, specific mention of Nicodemus, a figure from the New Testament who secretly visited Jesus. This man, with Joseph of Arimethea, will remove the body of Jesus from the cross, prepare it with oil, herbs, and spices, and then place it into the empty tomb. Okay. We can now go back to the beginning of the poem and, even if it's just a place to start, imagine that the scattering congregation includes the followers of Jesus. We know that these disciples wandered throughout the Mediterranean area spreading the Gospel after the resurrection and ascension, but in the days immediately following Christ's death, we also see them confused, grief stricken and huddled fearfully in a locked room (John 20:19).

This context can perhaps help us understand some of the images earlier in the poem, but as we will see, it will take us just so far. For instance, we can understand the fear that might be driving a disciple to sell his home prior to a hasty exit from town, and we could interpret the visitor as a nonbeliever, judging this home-seller for his lack of courage. We might even read the underground church bells as symbols for the disciples themselves, gone "underground," into hiding, starting at the slightest noise that might reveal them to the potentially hostile town folk. But there were no Christian churches in the time of Jesus, no cathedrals with vaulted ceilings or flying buttresses, no orderly rows of pews, no church bells. So the poet must intend some statement that will transcend the historic context suggested by the mention of Nicodemus.

Some additional information about Transtromer also helps: This Swedish poet recently won the Nobel Prize for literature. According to Robert Bly, the translator of this poem and a distinguished poet and author himself, Transtromer often employs what Bly calls the "deep image." While difficult to define (and Bly himself sometimes uses vague terminology when he speaks or writes of it), the term essentially means the use of words or phrases that tap into the Freudian subconscious to produce images we may not completely understand, like a dream that puzzles us upon waking. So while reading a poem written by Transtromer, we may expect to encounter relatively clear, accessible images (for example, comparing marble pillars of a church to the plaster cast around a broken arm), but also opaque, irrational images tapped from deep inside the poet or persona which many readers may find nearly incomprehensible. Not surprisingly, given the psychological origins of deep images, many of them have to do with interiority or suppression, with what lies deep inside or underneath.

Understanding even just this much about Transtromer helps us get a slightly firmer handle on parts of the poem. The word "inside" appears three times in "The Scattered Congregation," and in the first two stanzas we note clear contrasts between interiors and exteriors. In stanza 1, the "we" of the poem (note the plural persona maintained throughout) describes getting a home ready to show as if they were about to sell. An unspecified visitor, presumably a prospective buyer, apparently impressed with the house ("you live well"), speculates that the persona must be moving due to hidden reasons. The visitor contrasts outward appearance (an ordered, attractive house) with the hypothetical slum within, poor and chaotic. In stanza 2, the persona compares white marble pillars and vaulting of the church to a plaster cast around the "broken arm of faith." Again, we see an attractive exterior (beautiful, solid pillars and soaring vaulted ceilings) contrasted with a broken, damaged interior.

The next three lines present an image I have difficulty unpacking. The persona describes a begging bowl, perhaps a kind of alms basin, that "lifts from the floor / and floats along the pews." The persona places this image of ascension (lifting, floating) in contrast with the bells of the church in stanza 4, which have "gone underground," to a place below the worship space of the church. Given the context

of a fearful, scattered congregation, we grasp the metaphorical con-
notations of this phrase: just as the bells, which should sit high atop
a steeple and ring out proudly for all to hear, have gone underground,
so too the members of this worshipping community have fled public
sight. So I can wrap my mind around an understanding of stanza 4
now, and further, I can see the juxtaposing of the lofty bells being
brought down, so to speak, while the lowly begging bowl ascends
from the floor and floats through the air. Is the begging bowl sup-
posed to remind us of the slum from line 3? Are we meant to think of
a collection plate slowly passing among the pews? Is the image meant
to emphasize the emptiness of the pews now that the congregation
has scattered or gone underground? The image could mean any or all
of these things.

Nicodemus came by night: It intrigues me that the persona
describes Nicodemus as a "sleepwalker." We know that he came to
speak to Jesus by night so that others in the Jewish community would
not discover his highly suspicious activities. The New Testament offers
a clear delineation between his daytime occupation and what he did
after sunset. In a poem filled with contrasts between the internal and
the external, surely the figure of Nicodemus does not appear acciden-
tally. The persona contrasts a nice house with the slum inside, the
marble pillars with the broken arm inside the plaster cast, and the
begging bowl floating upward with the downward movement of the
church bells. Sleepwalking offers a similar juxtaposition, asleep while
appearing to be awake. What lies deep inside has taken control of
external actions.

Nicodemus was a powerful man, a rich, influential member of the
Sanhedrin, the ruling class, yet Jesus says to him, "unless one is born
anew, he cannot see the kingdom of God." Nicodemus seems confused
by this statement, so Jesus tries to clarify: "unless one is born of water
and the Spirit, he cannot enter the kingdom of God. That which is born
of the flesh is flesh, and that which is born of the Spirit is spirit" (John
3:3, 5–6). Jesus draws a clear distinction between physical birth and
the spiritual rebirth in baptism ("water and the Spirit"), a difference
surely relevant in a poem that offers such contrasts between exteriors
and interiors. As we will recall from "Making the House Ready for the
Lord," outward manifestations and actions (making the house shiny

and clean) matter less than the content of your heart (love for those in need). Various Bible passages frequently imply that this content is far from perfect. For instance, in Jeremiah we read "the heart is deceitful above all things, and desperately corrupt; who can understand it?" (17:9), and this from Genesis: "the imagination of a man's heart is evil from his youth" (8:21). The human heart, like the rest of fallen creation, requires vigilance, healing, and renewal.

Robert Bly, the poem's translator, has suggested that words like "slum" and "broken" imply the poem describes the decline of Christianity, and clearly there could be validity to this interpretation. References to "slums" inside and broken faith, church bells hanging from sewage pipes and empty pews powerfully suggest corruption, vacancy, and impotence. I might also suggest that words like "ring" and "float" complicate this interpretation of the poem. While perhaps true, as the visitor in the first stanza thinks, that "we" have a slum inside of us (these fallen, sinful, deceitful hearts of ours), hope might still come from the church. The persona may perceive the church's alabaster as a mere plaster cast around our "broken" faith, but the point of a cast is to *heal.*

Who's got the Address: While a scattering of a congregation carries negative connotations, the faith does not spread without its missioners and evangelists. As Jesus goes on to say to Nicodemus that night, "The wind blows where it will, and you hear the sound of it, but you do not know whence it comes or whither it goes; so it is with everyone who is born of the spirit" (John 3:8). This statement describes the unpredictably nomadic life of the Spirit. We do not know from where it will come or where it will go, nor can we predict where it will lead us or what we will be asked to do. So we do what we must, moving forward in faith, as the disciples did during the time of Nicodemus, which brings us back, again, to the poem's conclusion. Nicodemus is on his way to the Address. The persona asks who has the Address, and nobody seems to know. But it does not matter: "that's where we're going." Poet and scholar Peter Chou suggests in his poem, "What Is the Address," that the Address is heaven. Perhaps so, and certainly, on this day of all days, I will thankfully pause and recall that heaven has become a viable Address for me only because of Christ's sacrifice today. But the point may transcend Chou's understandable reaching for eternity. The persona does not ask *What is the Address?* but rather *Who's got the Address?* Nobody knows the answer to the question, but they will go just the same. We all bear a slum inside, flawed vessels holding imperfect hearts and broken faith, but perhaps we can carry within us also the sound of those church bells. And "whenever we take a step, they ring."

EASTER

"Heron Rises from the Dark, Summer Pond" by Mary Oliver (2002)

So heavy
is the long-necked, long-bodied heron,
always it is a surprise
when her smoke-colored wings   *line 4*

open
and she turns
from the thick water,
from the black sticks   *line 8*

of the summer pond,
and slowly
rises into the air
and is gone.   *line 12*

Then, not for the first or the last time,
I take the deep breath
of happiness, and I think
how unlikely it is   *line 16*

that death is a hole in the ground,
how improbable
that ascension is not possible,
though everything seems so inert, so nailed   *line 20*

back into itself—
the muskrat and his lumpy lodge,
the turtle,
the fallen gate.   *line 24*

And especially it is wonderful
that the summers are long
and the ponds so dark and so many,
and therefore it isn't a miracle   *line 28*

but the common thing,
this decision,
this trailing of the long legs in the water,
this opening up of the heavy body   *line 32*

into a new life: see how the sudden
gray-blue sheets of her wings
strive toward the wind; see how the clasp of nothing
takes her in.   *line 36*

You will find discussion questions for this poem on page 138.

Structure: This beautiful poem by Mary Oliver comprises three sections, three sentences really, clearly demarcated by three full stops. The first twelve lines offer a simple, though powerful, image of a blue heron slowly rising into the air from a dark summer pond. The second twelve lines turn inward as the persona considers death and what may lie beyond death. The final twelve lines return to the image of the heron, though by this point its flight has acquired a clear metaphorical, metaphysical dimension ("new life"). The length of the poem on the page and its thirty-six short centered lines visually reinforce the long neck, long body, long legs, and long flight described therein.

Also imbedded within the poem we may perceive a structural *chiasmus*, in which certain verbal elements are balanced, but reversed, in order to communicate that the image of the ascending heron has changed as it passes through the (literally) central idea of the persona: death does not represent a final ending, and ascension is possible.

> A. So **heavy** / is the long-necked, long-**bodied** heron
>> B. **open**
>>> C. from the **black** sticks /
>>>> D. of the **summer pond**
>>>>> E. **how unlikely** that *death* is a hole in the ground
>>>>> E. **how improbable** that *ascension* is not possible
>>>> D. that the **summers** are long / and the **ponds**
>>> C. so **dark**
>> B. this **opening** up
> A. of the **heavy body**

F. Into a **new life** . . . see . . . see.

Do you see this? We progress through certain words ("heavy . . . bodied" / "open" / "black" / "summer pond") to arrive at the central pairing of similar terms ("how unlikely" / "how improbable"). At this central point, *death* becomes *ascension*, and then we move through the same or similar words, but in reverse order ("summers" and "ponds" / "dark" / "opening" / "heavy body"). As I have lettered them above, the pattern is ABCDE : EDCBA. A mirror reflection; the same, yet different.

This brilliant structuring supports our understanding that the persona sees the rising of the heron in a new way after he takes a deep breath of happiness and meditates upon what he has observed. As death becomes ascension, the persona's understanding of the heron's long upward flight evolves. In lines 10–12, the heron "slowly / rises into the air / and is gone," but in lines 35–36, the persona encourages the reader to "see how the clasp of nothing / takes her in." The former description offers mere disappearance with no particular significance (akin to death if it *were* just "a hole in the ground"); the latter, though, offers a waiting agent, a "nothing," materially imperceptible perhaps, but there nonetheless, which clasps the heron and takes her in. We accompany the persona into the final four lines of the poem in witness of this "new life." The image of something or someone waiting above for the heron's arrival is so important that the persona exhorts us to pay attention. See? No mere vanishing this! See! *This* is ascension, an open-armed welcome. "Heron Rises from the Dark, Summer Pond" presents a wonderful example of form and content working in harmony to create meaning.

The fallen gate: Not only do many of the words and phrases in this poem point toward crucifixion and resurrection ("nailed," "ascension," "miracle," and "new life"), but much of the imagery also supports this theme. Note, for instance, how the shape of the heron (long-necked, long-bodied, trailing long legs, with wings outstretched) suggests a cross. I also think it's fantastic that the heron rises from water. The first time I read this poem I thought at once of a great passage from Romans: "Do you not know that all of us who have been baptized into Christ Jesus were baptized into his death? We were *buried* therefore with him *by baptism into death*, so that as Christ was *raised from the dead* by the glory of the Father, we too might walk in *newness of life*" (Romans 6:3–4; I've emphasized the terms particularly relevant to Oliver's poem). In this context, the poem encompasses not only death and ascension, but also baptism. In fact, the imagery of the poem (the summer ponds are "dark"; the water, "thick" and filled with "black sticks") actually foregrounds our understanding of baptism as a death, a grave in which we too are buried with Christ and from which we too ascend with him to walk in newness of life. I even love it that Oliver has chosen *ponds* as her body of water. The heron does not rise from the dark summer creek or the dark summer lake, she rises from a pond, a small, round pond, like a pool . . . or a font.

In the context of all this great stuff, one phrase, "the fallen gate," really pulled me up short the first couple of readings. Good heavens, to what does *this* refer? Jesus once described himself as a gate guarding the sheep (John 10), and so a fallen gate may suggest his apparent fall (death) upon the cross. That seems a little tenuous to me. The phrase follows two examples from nature of creatures who pull back: the muskrat retreats into her "lumpy lodge," and the turtle recoils into his shell. "The fallen gate" just doesn't fit into the same category; rather, it suggests that a way is now *open* that was formerly closed (note that "open" is the only word in the poem isolated on its own line for emphasis). Ultimately, the fallen gate reminds me of nothing more than the torn veil: "Therefore, brethren, since we have confidence to enter the sanctuary by the blood of Jesus, by the *new and*

The Harrowing of Hell: Jesus leads the Faithful who died before him out of Hell and into the Heavenly Kingdom. Note that the Gates of Hell have fallen into a cross under Christ's feet.

living way which he *opened* for us through the curtain, that is, through his flesh, . . . let us draw near with a true heart in full assurance of faith" (Hebrews 10:19–22; again, emphasis added). After reading this New Testament verse, I remembered also the Harrowing of Hell, the tradition which teaches us that on the Saturday between death and resurrection Jesus descended to the Realm of the Dead, breaking down the gates to release the righteous who had already died. As I've continued my research on this possibility, I've been delighted to discover that in the Eastern Orthodox Iconographic Tradition, we can find several examples of this triumphant visit to the underworld. In them, the Gates of Hell are often portrayed as falling into the shape of a cross, as what had been nailed shut has been permanently opened. Wow.

Ultimately then, "Heron Rises from the Dark, Summer Pond" returns us to the promise of eternity. Through baptism, death transcends a hole in the ground. Through Christ, ascension is possible. Christ's transcendence empowers us to overcome the leaden inertia of

our own mortality; our heavy bodies open up to this newness of life.[1]
As I have struggled over the past four years with illness and pain, grief
and depression, Mary Oliver's incredible poem has encouraged me to
think of these earthbound burdens as a variation on death and burial.
As I have felt the ceaseless weight of cancer bearing me down, as I
have experienced the inward spiraling of self-pity and anger, "Heron
Rises from the Dark, Summer Pond" reminds me that Christ is buried
with me. As I embrace the heavy darkness, I embrace also him. As
Christ was raised from death, so too shall I be, if I draw near him with
a true heart and in the full assurance of my faith. The persona declares
this belief with triumphant confidence. Take "the deep breath / of hap-
piness"! Strive toward the wind with joy, and in the end, believe that
the clasp of nothing will take you in at last.

---

1. Please refer back to Oliver's other poem in this collection, line 43 of "Such Singing in the
Wild Branches," for another juxtaposing of "open" and "heavy."

EASTER WEEK
"These spiritual windowshoppers"
by Rumi

These spiritual windowshoppers,
Who idly ask, *How much is that? Oh, I'm just looking.*
They handle a hundred items and put them down,
Shadows with no capital.   *line 4*

What is spent is love and two eyes wet with weeping,
But these walk into a shop,
And their whole lives pass suddenly in that moment,
In that shop.   *line 8*

Where did you go? "Nowhere."
What did you have to eat? "Nothing much."

Even if you don't know what you want,
Buy *something*, to be part of the exchanging flow.   *line 12*

Start a huge, foolish project,
Like Noah.   *line 14*

It makes absolutely no difference
What people think of you.   *line 16*

Another poem by Rumi

I would love to kiss you.
The price of kissing is your life.

Now my loving is running toward my life, shouting,
What a bargain, let's buy it.

Translations by Coleman Barks

You will find discussion questions for these two poems on page 139.

Rumi: Poet, mystic, and theologian, Jalal ad-Din Muhammad Balkhi (or Jalal ad-Din Muhammad Rumi) was born in what was then Persia in 1207 and died in 1273. We in the west usually identify him as simply "Rumi." He wrote thousands of lines of poetry, and some consider him the most popular poet in the world. I love his work for its (apparent) simplicity, sense of humor, and pure joy. For a straightforward yet profound lesson in faith, one can do no better than his poem "A Small Green Island." Look it up.

Window shopping: We all know spiritual window shoppers, people who drift idly through life, dabbling but seldom committing, apathetic. Just looking. Eating nothing much. Going nowhere in particular. Hoarding their love and avoiding risk. Rumi's persona has little patience with these people: "buy *something*," she admonishes. Join the exchanging flow that is life. As was the case in Shakespeare's "Sonnet 29," note that these poems by Rumi imagine love in capitalistic terms. Love brings "wealth" in the sonnet. Love represents the medium of exchange in "These Spiritual Windowshoppers." Meant to be spent, this expenditure ironically comes with its own cost, two eyes wet with weeping. To love, and to invest that love, comes with a price. *The price of kissing is your life.* The price of loving is your life.

The woman with the alabaster jar: Two days before Passover, Jesus was in the house of Simon the Leper. As he sat at the table, a woman approached him with an alabaster jar filled with nard, a very expensive ointment or perfumed oil. According to Matthew, this woman (unnamed in this version) poured the entire jar on his head. When the disciples witnessed this, they responded with indignation:

111

"Why this waste? For this ointment might have been sold for a large sum, and given to the poor." But Jesus does not see this action as wasteful at all: "Why do you trouble the woman?" he asks, "For she has done a beautiful thing to me" (Matthew 26:8–10). The woman with the alabaster jar holds back nothing. She spends it all, pours it all out, even as Jesus makes it clear that she performs it all in the context of inevitable death: "In pouring this ointment on my body she has done it to prepare me for burial" (Matthew 26:12). In anointing his body with the entire contents of her flask, this woman symbolically embraces Christ's death, and as she dies with him, so too will she participate in the new life to follow: "I say to you," Jesus concludes, "wherever this gospel is preached in the whole world, what she has done will be told in memory of her" (Matthew 26:13). Spend your passion, Rumi's persona cries. Lose your life.

A vital dimension of Lent includes recognizing and embracing loss. "Remember you are dust," we are told on the first day of the season, "and to dust you shall return." We often speak of what we intend to "give up" for Lent, what we are going to lose, if you will, for the duration of forty days. I also have plenty of friends who emphasize taking on something for Lent, trying out a ministry or experimenting with a new spiritual discipline, but even this taking on almost inevitably entails a giving up of something else. A new prayer ritual at dawn, for instance, might require postponing or foregoing entirely the newspaper or Facebook (or sleep) you might have enjoyed otherwise. As we move through Lent and into Holy Week and Easter, the focus shifts, I would say, to the joys and benefits of this losing, or this loving. If we start Lent saying "to dust I shall return," we conclude it with "He is risen!" Remember the remarkable message of "A prayer that will be answered"? "I know that I will suffer and die; I also know that my redeemer lives." Here we find the season of Lent, writ small.

To love is to lose: to lose your heart, to lose control, to lose your dignity, to lose yourself. Elizabeth Bishop writes of this. "Lose something every day," her persona exhorts. "Now practice losing farther, losing faster." Lose with abandon; spend your passion with exuberance. The price of kissing is indeed your life, but your life was not yours to begin with. Hold back from spending your love and you reduce your risk of pain, but what kind of life is this? Rumi's persona assures us that the world does not need cautious spectators. It needs spendthrifts. It needs gamblers who will place all their eggs in one basket and fishermen who will drop their nets. It needs people who will launch huge, foolish projects, unafraid of what others might think. It needs more women with alabaster jars.

One of the most surprising things about "These spiritual windowshoppers" is the abrupt appearance of Noah. I mean, seriously, does he not just come out of nowhere? Just as with *The Castle of Perseverance*, we suddenly perceive the presence of God, and what had seemed a mere secular piece on apathy or fear suddenly acquires the tinge of faith. To paraphrase the Stage Manager from *Our Town*, only poets and saints realize their lives "every, every minute," but we have it within us to be a saint like Noah. So, Rumi's persona cries, "Be a saint like Noah!" Recall the message of Rae Armantrout's "Advent." You are an author, a sculptor, a musician: your faith is your work in progress. Take on this "huge, foolish project," this act of creation which is living a life of faith. Baptist minister and civil rights leader Howard Thurman once wrote: "Don't ask yourself what the world needs; ask yourself what makes you come alive. Because what the world needs is people who have come alive." Rumi's poems communicate almost exactly the same thing. Wake up. Come to life. Follow your passion. Don't check with the world first. Listen to the voice of God. "Forget your life," Rumi has written elsewhere. "Say God is great. Get up!"

I return again and again to the exuberant moments in all of these poems. The soaring spirit of the persona in Shakespeare's "Sonnet 29" when she remembers she is loved ("For thy sweet love remembered such wealth brings, / That then I scorn to change my state with kings"). The persona of "Love Poem" embracing his awkwardly graceful beloved ("So gaily in love's unbreakable heaven / Our souls on glory of spilt bourbon float"). The exhortation towards epiphany in "Such singing in the wild branches" ("Listen, everyone has a chance . . . open the door and fly on your heavy feet"). Rumi's "loving" running towards life shouting "What a bargain! Let's buy it!" These poems teach us that spirits soar when we refuse to be nailed back down into our finite existence, our lumpy lodges or our turtle shells, our inevitable fears and failings, or by the heaviness, sickness, and disease inherent in our material bodies. Flawed, faulty, and fallen, we have yet the capacity to love, and we cherish hope. We look up. We reach for eternity. Over and over in these poems we see these qualities represented by upward movement, images of daybreak, by new life and rebirth. Even in our darkest, most Ecclesiastical moments of bitterness or despair, our poets remind us that we have reason to rejoice and assure us that miracles are common things. Expect them . . . like Noah. Go forth. Seek them out. In this expenditure of love, in this exuberant embrace of humanity with all its failings, we have before us the perfect model. "For God so loved the world that he gave his only Son, that whoever believes in him should not perish but have eternal life" (John 3:16). Ask Jesus, and he will tell you: *the price of loving is your life.*

Chapel Hill, North Carolina.
Draft completed on April 18, 2014. Good Friday.
And third anniversary of cancer diagnosis.

Therefore, surrounded as we are with such a vast cloud of witnesses, let us fling aside every encumbrance and the sin that so readily entangles our feet. And let us run with patient endurance the race that lies before us. (Hebrews 12:1, Weymouth New Testament)

It is a good life, Hazel Grace. (The Fault in Our Stars, by John Green)

At first, you will think there are good days and there are bad days; later, you will realize that they are all good days. (Brian, my therapist)

A Glossary of Poetic Terms

Alliteration: The repetition of an initial consonant (usually) or vowel (sometimes) in a sequence of words or syllables. These lines from John Donne's "Holy Sonnet 14" offer an explosively wonderful example of alliteration:

> "bend / Your force, to break, blow, burn, and make me new."

Allusion: A reference in one text to a person, object, or event in another text or from history. For instance, line 2 of "The Donkey" ("And figs grew upon thorn") is an allusion to a Bible verse:

> "Figs are not gathered from thorns" (Luke 6:44).

Assonance: The repetition of vowel sounds in a sequence of words or syllables. The final two lines of "Those Winter Sundays" by Robert Hayden represent a superb example of assonance:

> "What did I know, what did I know / of love's austere and lonely offices?"

Some scholars would argue that the repetition of the initial vowel sound in "of," "austere," and "offices" actually amounts to *alliteration*. This kind of controversy will bring English professors to blows at departmental sherries. Don't even get us started on the Oxford comma.

Caesura: A strong pause or break in the middle of a line of poetry. Line 12 of Percy Bysshe Shelly's "Ozymandias" contains a dramatic caesura:

> "My name is Ozymandias, king of kings:
> Look on my works ye Mighty, and despair!"
> Nothing beside remains. Round the decay . . . (lines 10–12)

Chiasmus: A pattern in which words, phrases, or sentences are repeated, but in reverse order. This line from John F. Kennedy's inauguration speech contains chiasmus:

> "Ask not what **your country** can do for **you; ask what you** can do for **your country**."

Sophisticated chiasmus usually suggests change or transformation.

Consonance: A repetition of consonant sounds other than at the beginnings of words (see *alliteration*). Lines 2 and 3 of Robert Hayden's "Those Winter Sundays" feature both consonance and alliteration:

> and put his clothes on in the **blueblack c**old,
> then with **cr**a**ck**ed hands that a**ched**

Some critics will argue that it is not true consonance unless two or more consonants are repeated, with a different vowel sound between them, like **fier**ce and **for**ce: I think that's too narrow a definition. This opinion sometimes gets me ejected from English Department sherries (see *assonance*).

Couplet: Two consecutive lines of poetry that rhyme.

End-stopped: A line of poetry in which the end of a sentence or clause coincides with the end of the line. Such lines usually end with a punctuation mark signaling a pause in the reading.

Enjambment: Also called **run-on lines,** these lines of poetry do not end with any punctuation, and the sense or meaning of the line carries over into the next line of poetry. The middle line of the following excerpt from Shakespeare's "Sonnet 29" demonstrates enjambment:

> Haply I think on thee, and then my state,
> Like to the lark at break of day arising
> From sullen earth, sings hymns at heaven's gate;

Foreshadowing: A technique through which something later in a literary work is indicated by material earlier in that same work. For example, in the Christmas poem "Bezhetsk," line 2 ("The cornflower eyes of my son are blossoming there") foreshadows the birth of Christ alluded to later in the poem.

Internal rhyme: Rhyme that occurs in a poem other than at the ends of the lines. In line 5 of "Those Winter Sundays" (". . . banked fires blaze. No one ever thanked him"), "banked" and "thanked" represent internal rhyme.

Juxtapose: To place two or more things side by side in order to compare or contrast them. See the juxtaposing of "open" and "heavy" in "Heron Rises from the Dark, Summer Pond" by Mary Oliver.

Liminal: On a threshold in time or place. Literary works featuring thresholds, doors, windows, fences, borders, etc., demonstrate liminality. Liminal times include dawn, dusk, and midnight. Liminality often features prominently in works about transition or change.

Memento mori: A Latin phrase that means "remember you will die"; a symbolic or artistic reminder of the inevitability of death.

Octave: The first eight lines of a sonnet. Lots of different options as far as organization and rhyme patterns are concerned: see *sonnet*.

Oxford comma: The comma directly in front of a coordinating conjunction in a series or list of three or more items. For instance, in the phrase "red, white, and blue," the second comma, the one right before "and," is the Oxford comma. Manuals of style and usage differ widely as to whether using this comma is correct or incorrect. Oh, this has almost nothing to do with poetry: I just wanted you all to know what you have missed by not being English majors (though please note that no less a figure than John Donne *does use* the Oxford comma: see *alliteration*).

Persona: A character created by the author through whom the narrative is expressed. See more details on pages 9–10.

Quatrain: A *stanza* of four lines, with any number of possible rhyme schemes.

Sestet: Generally, any poem or *stanza* six lines long; specifically, the final six lines of an Italian sonnet.

Sonnet: A structured poem fourteen lines long. The sonnet exists in two historic forms: the Italian sonnet and the English or Shakespearean sonnet. The Italian sonnet consists of two *quatrains* (often called an *octave*) and a *sestet*. The Shakespearean sonnet is divided into three *quatrains* and a concluding *couplet*.

The Italian form is the older of the two, its introductory *octave* often posing a question or establishing a position that is then answered or resolved in the *sestet*. Early English practitioners of the form rendered the last two lines into a *couplet* (the first four lines of the Italian sestet evolved into a third *quatrain*). The result is a versatile form, in which the three quatrains can be in relation to each other in a number of different ways and the epigrammatic couplet can summarize, extend, or reverse what has preceded it. Most of the earliest sonnets were concerned with the persona's relationship with a love object, and love—in all its restless variety—remains a primary subject of the sonnet into the twenty-first century.

Stanza: A repeated grouping of two or more lines of poetry, similar in line length, rhythm, and rhyme pattern. The form of "The Donkey," for instance, is four 4-line stanzas.

Triplet or Tercet: Three consecutive lines of poetry that rhyme (usually a single rhyme, but sometimes an alternating *aba*).

Villanelle: A highly structured poem, nineteen lines long, consisting of five tercets (or *triplets*) and one *quatrain*. The first line of the poem is repeated as the last line of the second and fourth triplets. The third line of the poem (which must rhyme with the first line) is repeated as the last line of the third and fifth triplets. The first and third lines must also be the last two lines of the poem.

The rhyming pattern of a villanelle is also very repetitive; in fact, a villanelle has only two rhyme endings: the *a*-rhyme repeats thirteen times (in "One Art" that's the "master/disaster" rhyme), and the *b*-rhyme repeats six times (that's the "intent/spent" rhyme). The rhyme pattern of the triplets must be *aba*, and the rhyme scheme for the final quatrain is *abaa*.

Rather complicated, isn't it?

How did such a repetitive form originate? One charming theory states that the form started as a harvest-time call and response song, and the term *villanelle* does indeed derive from the Italian *villanella* (rustic song), which in turn is related to *villano* (peasant or farmhand) or *villa* (farm or country house). The earliest printed villanelles, in French, focus on pastoral themes (romanticized, idyllic country life) or pastoral lyric (use of pastoral themes to portray death and loss). Love and loss continue to be primary themes in contemporary villanelles, though innovative artists have expanded the uses of the form; for instance, Elizabeth Bishop's "One Art" explores loss, but she develops her theme in delightfully unexpected ways through variations on the repeated lines.

Discussion Questions

Discussion Questions for George Herbert's "The Collar"

1. How would you describe the persona's attitude in this poem? What seems to be her problem? With whom does she have a grievance?

2. How does the persona's attitude change by the final four lines of the poem? Why does it change?

3. Along with the above question, note that the rhyme scheme is irregular, to say the least, until line 33. Why do you think a regular pattern is resolved in the final four lines of the poem?

4. Note that several of the shorter lines stack up over each other to create a straight line or margin through the center of the poem (look at, for instance, how lines 16, 18, 22, and 25 are all aligned with each other). Any ideas as to why Herbert would structure the poem this way?

5. Read the following and then explain if or how this biblical passage has an impact on your understanding of the poem:

   > In Galatians, Paul writes: "God is not mocked, for whatever a man sows, that he will also reap. For he who sows to his own flesh will from the flesh reap corruption; but he who sows to the Spirit will from the Spirit reap eternal life. And let us not grow weary in well-doing, for in due season we shall reap, if we do not lose heart" (6:7–9).

6. To what does the title of the poem refer? Say the title out loud one last time: "The Collar." Now, read the last two lines out loud. Do you hear the echo? How does it change the orientation of the poem if we think of its title as "The Caller"?

Discussion Questions for Shakespeare's "Sonnet 29"

1. How would you describe the persona's attitude in the first eight lines of the poem? How does her attitude change beginning with line 9? Why does it change?

2. Look at the ends of all the lines of the sonnet: what is different about the end of line 11? Look up *enjambment*. Why do we see enjambment at the end of line 11?

3. How does it change your understanding of the poem to read "thee" in line 10 as referring to God? Is there sufficient context (in your opinion) to justify a religious or spiritual interpretation of the poem? Why or why not?

4. Resolved: the most important word in the poem is "remembered" from line 13 ("For thy sweet love **remembered** such wealth brings"). Discuss.

5. Read the following and then explain if or how this biblical passage has an impact on your understanding of the poem:

> "Who shall separate us from the love of Christ? Shall trouble or hardship or persecution or famine or nakedness or danger or sword? . . . No, in all these things we are more than conquerors through him who loved us. For I am convinced that neither death nor life, neither angels nor demons, neither the present nor the future, nor any powers, neither height nor depth, nor anything else in all creation, will be able to separate us from the love of God that is in Christ Jesus our Lord" (Romans 8:35–39, NIV). Paul assures us that no material conditions, indeed, nothing in all creation, can separate us from Christ's love, but Shakespeare's "Sonnet 29" suggests an answer to Paul's initial question: nobody can separate us from the love of God . . . except *us*.

Discussion questions for John Frederick Nims's "Love Poem"

1. In the first eight lines of the poem, pay particular attention to the rhythms of the lines and the poet's use of *enjambment* and *caesura*. Why do you suppose the poet creates such rollicking rhythms?

2. The persona uses vocabulary one might not ordinarily expect to see in a love poem: "clumsiest," "shipwreck," "fidgeting," and "unpredictable" offer good examples. These surprising terms (and others) create what effect(s) in the poem?

3. Related to the above, perhaps, how would you describe the persona? What is his tone? What is his attitude toward the one he loves?

4. Describe how the world of the poem expands in stanzas 4 and 5. What is the effect of this momentary switch from first person singular to first person plural?

5. Read the following and then explain if or how this biblical passage has an impact on your understanding of the poem:

> The Bible is filled with deeply flawed human beings. Exodus offers us an early example: "Moses said to the Lord, 'Oh, my Lord, I am not eloquent, either heretofore or since thou hast spoken to thy servant; but I am slow of speech and tongue.' Then the Lord said to him, 'Who makes him dumb, or deaf, or seeing, or blind? Is it not I, the Lord? Now therefore go, and I will be with your mouth and teach you what you shall speak'" (Exodus 4:10–12). God has a long and distinguished history of choosing imperfect people (as if there were any other kind) to do his work, and the beloved in this poem takes her place among them.

Discussion questions for Mary Oliver's "Making the House Ready for the Lord

1. How would you describe the persona's attitude at the beginning of this poem? What seems to be his dilemma?

2. How has the persona's attitude evolved by the final five lines of the poem? Why has it changed?

3. As you read the poem carefully, you probably noticed several words and phrases get repeated: "it is the season," for instance, and "what shall I do." Although the poem looks perfectly well balanced on the page (all the lines are about the same length and every other line is indented), it is clearly not structured to emphasize the word patterns. Why do you think this is so?

4. Could the idea of "making the house ready" carry any metaphorical significance?

5. As Paul describes his conversion to Christianity, he says he hears "a voice saying to me 'Saul, Saul, why do you persecute me?' And I answered, 'Who are you, Lord?' And he said to me, 'I am Jesus of Nazareth whom you are persecuting.' . . . And I said, 'What shall I do, Lord?'" (Acts 22:7–10). In this context, how many different ways could we understand "what shall I do?" in this poem?

6. Read the following and then explain if or how this biblical passage has an impact on your understanding of the poem:

   > Matthew, chapter 25, Jesus teaches the disciples that, in order to "inherit the kingdom prepared for you," they must reach out to those in need. "For I was hungry and you gave me food," Jesus says, "I was thirsty and you gave me drink, I was a stranger and you welcomed me, I was naked and you clothed me, I was sick and you visited me, I was in prison and you came to me. . . . as you did it to one of the least of these my brethren, you did it to me" (34–40).

Discussion questions for Thomas Hardy's "The Oxen"

1. Note the effective way the persona describes, in just a few words, a faith community in the first eight lines. How would you describe this community?

2. Lines 9 and 10 mark a clear transition in the poem. What changes? Note, for example, the change in first-person pronouns: what is the significance of this switch?

3. How would you describe the attitude of the persona toward the faith community she recalls from her childhood? What is her attitude toward faith in general in the present time?

4. How does it impact a reading to recall that Hardy wrote the poem during World War I?

5. Read the following and then explain if or how this biblical encounter has an impact on your understanding of the poem:

> When the disciple Thomas hears the news about the resurrection, he says: "Unless I see in his hands the wound made by the nails and put my finger into the wound, and put my hand into his side, I will never believe." During their encounter afterward, Jesus says to him: "Because you have seen me, you have believed. Blessed are those who have not seen and yet have believed" (John 20:25, 29, Weymouth New Testament). We, like the persona in "The Oxen," are those who have not seen. We have not seen the miracle in Cana. We have not seen the empty tomb. We have not seen the spear wound in the side of the risen Lord. We have not seen the oxen kneel at midnight.

Discussion questions for Anna Akhmatova's "Bezhetsk"

1. We do not realize until line 6 that the persona is recalling the town specifically at Christmastime: how do you read any of the first lines differently after you know this?

2. Given that the poem is set in winter, why the two early references to flowers?

3. The persona describes memory as "stern" and "ungiving" now, but in *Bezhetsk* memory also throws open her doors with a low bow. What does this image suggest? What do you think it means that the persona would not go through those doors, but instead slams them closed again?

4. Anna Akhmatova, born in 1889, lived much of her life under the Soviet Regime. In that context, do you believe there is any particular significance attached to the word "sickle" in line 4?

5. Read the following and then explain if or how this biblical passage has an impact on your understanding of the poem:

> In his second letter to the Corinthians, Paul writes of the difficulty of maintaining faith during a time of trial: "We have this treasure in earthen vessels, to show that the transcendent power belongs to God and not to us. We are afflicted in every way, but not crushed; perplexed, but not driven to despair; persecuted, but not forsaken; struck down, but not destroyed" (4:7–9). Akhmatova's "Bezhetsk" is about loss, what the village has lost and what the persona has lost, yet the poem also participates in the paradox articulated by Paul.

Discussion questions for T.S. Eliot's "The Journey of the Magi"

1. Early in the poem, the persona establishes the time of year as "The very dead of winter," yet two lines later he describes camels "Lying down in the melting snow" (suggesting a spring thaw?) and four lines later mentions "summer palaces." What is the point of this seasonal slipperiness?

2. At Christmastime, what do we expect voices in the air to be singing? Lines 19 and 20 pull the rug out from under that expectation: According to the persona, what were the voices *really* singing? What does this reveal about the persona?

3. The middle section of the poem is filled with biblical *allusions*; what is the significance of:

   • Three trees on a low sky
   • A tavern with vine-leaves over the lintel
   • Pieces of silver
   • Feet kicking the empty wine-skins

   How does an understanding of these allusions have an impact on your reading of this poem?

4. Line 25 may be a reference to The White Horse of Uffington, a white figure of a horse carved into the countryside as early as one thousand years before the birth of Christ. Over three hundred feet long, the horse is comparable in design to other horse figures in Celtic Art and on Celtic coins. What is the significance of this figure in this poem?

5. Describe the persona's attitude toward this entire experience. Near the end, he assures us that he "would do it again, *but*. . . ." (emphasis added). Do you believe him? Why or why not?

6. Related to the above, the persona tells us in his final line that he "should be glad of another death." Whose death? How, if at all, might it change your understanding of that final line (or

even of the poem as a whole) to remember this verse from "We Three Kings":

> Myrrh is mine, its bitter perfume
> Breathes a life of gathering gloom;
> Sorrowing, sighing, bleeding, dying,
> Sealed in the stone cold tomb

Discussion questions for Mary Oliver's
"Such Singing in the Wild Branches"

1. Of what significance is the word "finally" in line 2?

2. Lines 11–29 comprise a single, long, complicated sentence. Why? How would you describe the persona's attitude in this section of the poem? What do you make of his repeated use of the verb "seemed"?

3. The motion or energy of much of the poem is upward (see, for instance, lines 13, 20, and 21). Why is that? Of what significance is the isolated word "stopped" (line 18)?

4. In the last six lines of the poem, the persona suddenly addresses his audience. Why is it important to him to do so? What does it add to the experience of the poem?

5. Read the following and then explain if or how this biblical passage has an impact on your understanding of the poem:

> "Since we have such a hope, we are very bold, not like Moses, who put a veil over his face so that the Israelites might not see the end of the fading splendor. But their minds were hardened; for to this day, when they read the old covenant, that same veil remains unlifted, because only through Christ is it taken away. . . . for when a man turns to the Lord the veil is removed. . . . and we all, with unveiled faces, beholding the glory of the Lord, are being changed into his likeness from one degree of glory to another" (2 Corinthians 3:13–18).

6. Consider how these two lines, from a couple of contemporary novels, could enhance our thematic understanding of "Such Singing in the Wild Branches":

> "You gave me a forever within the numbered days, and I'm grateful."
>
> —*The Fault in Our Stars*, by John Green, page 260

> "Because from now on, for you, I'll be searching for those moments of always within never."
>
> —*The Elegance of the Hedgehog*, by Muriel Barbery, page 325

Discussion questions for Percy Bysshe Shelley's "Ozymandias

1. After the first ten words, the rest of the poem is actually the speaker's quotation of a different person, the traveler from an antique land. What is the effect of this second-hand description of the colossal wreck in the desert?

2. Note the sounds of the poem. Several word pairs are linked by alliteration and consonance (**st**one and **st**and; **c**old and **c**omman**d**, etc.). Notice also how many words rhyme with the third syllable of the name Ozy**mand**ias (land, stand, sand, hand, command). Why does the entire poem echo its title?

3. One of the most striking things about the poem is the seeming lack of value judgment: we are offered a description with no analysis, no "moral of the story." Is it possible to discern the persona's attitude towards what has been described to him? If so, what is it and how do you know?

4. A *caesura* is a strong stop (like a period or an exclamation point) in the middle of a line of poetry. The final five lines of the poem contain a powerful *caesura*: where is it and what is its effect?

5. Read the following and then explain if or how this biblical passage has an impact on your understanding of the poem:

   From the apocryphal book of Sirach: "Arrogance is hateful before the Lord and before men . . . How can he who is dust and ashes be proud? For even in life, his body decays. A long illness baffles the physician; the king of today will die tomorrow" (10:7a, 9–10).

Discussion questions for Elizabeth Bishop's "One Art"

1. What has the speaker of the poem lost? List all the losses, in the order the speaker presents them, through line 15. What does this list suggest about the speaker's experience with, and attitude toward, loss?

2. "One Art" is a villanelle,[1] a form that demands highly stylized repetition. Given the subject of the poem (loss), what is the effect of this repetition?

3. Bishop follows the rules of a villanelle and repeats line 1 as lines 6 and 12. But instead of repeating it exactly at line 18, it changes. What is meaningful about this change?

4. In fact, there are a lot of different things going on in that final stanza. For instance, what do you make of those two parenthetical comments? And what's up with that dash at the beginning of line 16?

5. Read the following and then explain if or how these biblical passages have an impact on your understanding of the poem:

   > "All things come of thee, and of thine own have we given thee. For we are strangers before thee, and sojourners, as were all our fathers: our days on the earth are as a shadow, and there is none abiding." (1 Chronicles 29:14–15)

   > Whoever loves his life too much in this world loses it, but whoever hates his life in this world will keep his life in eternity. (a slight paraphrase of John 12:25)

---

1. A **villanelle** is nineteen lines long, consisting of five 3-line stanzas and one 4-line stanza. The first line of the poem is repeated as the last line of the second and fourth stanzas. The third line of the poem (which must rhyme with the first line) is repeated as the last line of the third and fifth stanzas. These same two lines also make up the last two lines of the poem. The rhyme scheme must be *aba*, and the rhyme scheme for the last stanza is *abaa*.

Discussion questions for John Donne's "Holy Sonnet 14"

1. What is the persona's attitude throughout the sonnet? What is she asking God to do, and why?

2. We perceive an image in the first quatrain of a blown glass vessel or pottery that must be destroyed and then made anew. The violent language is accentuated by the alliteration of verbs like batter, break, and burn: Do you find this violence appropriate? Why or why not?

3. In the second quatrain the speaker imagines herself as a town, occupied by the "enemy," but wanting to be occupied by God. How (if at all) does the following passage have an impact on your understanding of what otherwise seems a rather random simile?

> In Lamentations, Jerusalem is portrayed as a woman who has been unfaithful: "Jerusalem sinned grievously, therefore she became filthy; . . . she took no thought of her doom; therefore her fall is terrible. . . . O Lord, behold my affliction, for the enemy has triumphed!" (1:8-9). Of course, we cannot forget that Jerusalem welcomed Jesus on Palm Sunday, only to crucify him days later: "Jerusalem, Jerusalem," Jesus cries, "killing the prophets and stoning those who are sent to you!" (Luke 13:34).

4. In the final three lines, the persona returns to the sense of paradox that has run throughout the poem: destroy me that I may be made new; enthrall me that I may be free; ravish me that I may be spiritually pure. In Romans, Paul writes: "We know that our old self was crucified with [Christ] so that the sinful body might be destroyed, and we might no longer be enslaved to sin" (6:6). How does it alter our understanding of this poem as we absorb the idea Paul expresses here, that we are slaves to our own sinfulness?

5. In lines 9–12, the sonnet participates in the "Christ as Bridegroom/ Church as Bride" metaphor familiar to us all, but Donne chooses to venture into the intimacy that is always suggested by this union. "Take me to you," implores the speaker, and in a context of violent imagery it is not inappropriate to note that for Donne's audience,

"ravish" was also synonymous with "rape." Does this extreme language just go too far? Why or why not?

6. Resolved: the most important line in the poem is, ". . . for you / As yet but knock, breathe, shine, and seek to mend" (lines 2–3), because it undercuts the violent extremity we see expressed elsewhere in the sonnet. Discuss.

Discussion questions for Anna Kamieńska's "A prayer that will be answered"

1. When a poem begins with "Lord, let me suffer much / and then let me die," the reader can be forgiven for dismissing the whole thing as a relentless downer. Is it? (Hint: This is a leading question. I think the poem offers some hope to alleviate the darkness—so the real question is, "Do you agree?").

2. How do you interpret line 3? What is this "walk through the quiet"?

3. Epictetus, ancient Greek philosopher, once wrote: "Let death be daily before your eyes, and you will never entertain any abject thought, nor too eagerly covet anything." Does this stoic statement alter in any way your attitude toward this poem?

4. The poem ends on what can be seen as a whimsical non sequitur: the poem is compared to a windowpane, "against which a stray bee bumps his head." Why do you think the poem ends on this note?

5. Read the following and then explain if or how this biblical passage has an impact on your understanding of the poem:

   "You intended to harm me," Joseph says to his brothers, "but God intended it for good to accomplish what is now being done, the saving of many lives. So then, don't be afraid. I will provide for you and your children" (Genesis 50:19–21, NIV). Joseph could see that, while the world is filled with hatred, jealousy, betrayal, and injustice, God works to bend all those human frailties to his good purposes.

6. Consider how these two excerpts from the journals of Anna Kamienska enhance our thematic understanding of "A prayer that will be answered":

   "A tomb is a gate. No one saw Christ rise from the dead. With good reason."

   "I pray in words; I pray in poems. I want to learn to pray through breathing, through dreams and sleeplessness, through love and renunciation. I pray in snow that falls outside the window. I pray in tears that do not end."

Discussion questions for G. K. Chesterton's "The Donkey"

1. Why does the poet choose to set this poem within a context that includes fish that fly and trees that walk? Consider that the presence of the donkey was foretold: "Rejoice greatly, O daughter of Zion! Shout aloud, O daughter of Jerusalem! Lo, your king comes to you; triumphant and victorious is he, humble, and riding on an ass" (Zechariah 9:9).

2. Why does the persona (the donkey) describe herself as "the devil's walking parody"? How would you describe the persona's tone throughout?

3. Stanza 3: Who else was scorned and derided? Who else kept silent when questioned?

4. What do you think is the secret referenced in line 12?

5. Who are the "fools" referenced in the final stanza?

6. The donkey literally bears the burden of Christ. Read the following and then explain if or how this biblical passage has an impact on your understanding of the poem:

   "Come to me, all who labor and are heavy laden, and I will give you rest. Take my yoke upon you, and learn from me, for I am gentle and lowly in heart, and you will find rest for your souls. For my yoke is easy, and my burden is light." (Matthew 11:28–30)

Discussion questions for Robert Hayden's "Those Winter Sundays"

1. Why is the word "too" important in line 1?

2. Early in the poem, we hear lots of hard "t" and "d" sounds: blue-black, cracked, ached, banked, thanked. How are these sounds relevant to the first six lines?

3. In line 5, the persona says that "no one ever thanked him." How does he *know* that no one else in the family ever thanked his father? If he can't really know, then what is he really saying in this line?

4. The persona writes that he fears the "chronic angers of that house." This thought is never developed. Are there any clues that might illuminate what might cause these chronic angers? If we accept that a house cannot literally be angry, why does the persona choose to phrase this line this particular way?

5. What is the final detail in the poem that seems to tip the persona's emotional state to acknowledgment and regret?

6. Read the following and then explain if or how this biblical passage has an impact on your understanding of the poem:

> [Jesus] came to Simon Peter; and Peter said to him, "Lord, do you wash my feet?" Jesus answered him, "What I am doing you do not know now, but afterward you will understand." . . . When he had washed their feet, and taken his garments, and resumed his place, he said to them, "Do you know what I have done to you? You call me Teacher and Lord, and you are right, for so I am. If I then, your Lord and Teacher, have washed your feet, you also ought to wash one another's feet. For I have given you an example, that you also should do as I have done to you." (John 13:6–15)

7. What is significant about the use of the word "offices" at the end of the poem?

8. Why is the poem called "Those Winter Sundays"? What are the connotations of winter? Of Sunday? Why "those" instead of "that" or "these"?

Discussion questions for Tomas Transtromer's "The Scattered Congregation"

1. Who is showing their home, and why? Why does the visitor think these home-sellers must have a "slum" inside of them?
2. What kind of attitude is suggested by a phrase like "the broken arm of faith"?
3. The word "inside" appears three times: to what extent is the contrast between interiors and exteriors important to an understanding of the poem?
4. Why have the church bells "gone underground"? What are the connotations of going underground?
5. Does the reference to Nicodemus provide a helpful context for understanding what has come before? Which congregation was scattered in the wake of Christ's crucifixion?

> Jesus once said to Nicodemus: "The wind blows where it will, and you hear the sound of it, but you do not know whence it comes or whither it goes; so it is with everyone who is born of the spirit." (John 3:8)

6. What does the final line reveal about this persona?

Discussion questions for Mary Oliver's
"Heron Rises from the Dark, Summer Pond"

1. Note that the poem is center-justified. Does its shape on the page suggest anything to you?

2. The poem can be divided into three equal parts (three sentences, really): lines 1–12, lines 13–24, and lines 25–36. How would you describe each of those sections?

3. The persona describes the heron's disappearance two different ways (lines 10–12 and lines 33–36). How do these descriptions differ? What has happened in between the two descriptions that might help us understand the difference?

4. Why is the word "open" on a line by itself? Consider if the following passage gives you any insight:

   > Therefore, brethren, since we have confidence to enter the sanctuary by the blood of Jesus, by the new and living way which he opened for us through the curtain, that is, through his flesh, . . . let us draw near with a true heart in full assurance of faith. (Hebrews 10:19–22)

5. The persona offers a series of examples of things that seem "inert" or "nailed back" into themselves. The muskrat hiding in his lumpy lodge and the turtle withdrawing into her shell make sense, but what about "the fallen gate"? How does that fit? What does it mean?

6. What do the summer ponds symbolize? What is the metaphorical significance of the heron's ascension?

7. Read the following and then explain if or how this biblical passage has an impact on your understanding of the poem:

   > Do you not know that all of us who have been baptized into Christ Jesus were baptized into his death? We were buried therefore with him by baptism into death, so that as Christ was raised from the dead by the glory of the Father, we too might walk in newness of life. (Romans 6:3–4)

Discussion questions for Rumi's
"These spiritual windowshoppers"

1. The persona describes spiritual window shoppers as "shadows with no capital," exhorting them to "buy *something*." Why imagine spiritual and/or emotional commitment in financial terms?

2. Explain how the lives of the spiritual window shoppers are encapsulated by lines 9–10.

3. The metaphor shifts after line 12 from parsimony to peer pressure: "start a huge, foolish project," the persona cries. "It makes absolutely no difference / What people think of you." What is the effect of this shift?

4. How does the mention of Noah change the poem?

5. How, if at all, does a reading of the second poem impact your understanding of the first? We return to a financial metaphor, but the persona of the second poem is clearly not a window shopper!

6. Read the following and then explain if or how this biblical passage has an impact on your understanding of the poem:

> "Be watchful, stand firm in your faith, be courageous, be strong. Let all that you do be done in love." (1 Corinthians 16:13–14)

Permissions Acknowledgments